A view of the Blue House from an original drawing by Abraham Crocker dated September 1786.

My thanks to Michael McGarvie for this information. Ed

The cake at the Society's 60th anniversary celebration, October 2018, made by The Old Bakehouse, Frome

FOREWORD

I came to Frome in 2012 and soon joined the Frome Society which had given me a warm welcome both during the summer visits and at the winter lectures. I soon realised the high quality of both these activities and the amount of hard work that goes into making them a success. When I became Chairman this year, I wanted to consider what I could bring to benefit FSLS from my background as a social worker. I had pursued a long career mainly with children and families; there were times of stress and difficulty but also successes when I was able to help families and young people turn round their lives. Unfortunately, I had to retire suddenly, in my mid-fifties due to a haemorrhage behind my right eye which affected my sight.

Starting with the *status quo,* I looked at what FSLS had done over those seven years in addition to the visits and lectures, which provide a social meeting point for both longstanding and new members. FSLS had published two new books: *The Butler and Tanner Story* by Lorraine Johnson and *Woad to This* by Carolyn Griffiths, seven Yearbooks, and republished five: *The Book of Frome* and *Frome Street and Place-Names* by Michael McGarvie, *The Buildings of Frome* by Rodney Goodall, *A History of Mells* by FW Cleverdon and *The Frome Heritage Trail* edited by Alastair MacLeay together with financial support given to Home in Frome to publish *Working Memories.*

FSLS had arranged regular lectures and talks during the Frome Festival at Rook Lane Chapel and the Merlin Theatre, which have been extremely successful. There had been three week-long study tours to Essex/Suffolk, the Potteries and Cornwall organised by members. The Frome and District Civic Society had continued to play a major role in the planning process for the town, particularly with the redevelopment of the Saxonvale and Garsdale area. I look forward to supporting similar activities in the future and would like to see FSLS carrying out more original research, which will give an opportunity to our newer members. I hope that FSLS will work closely with Frome Museum and other heritage and cultural organisations in Frome.

There were two major events in the year: The Frome Society celebrated its diamond jubilee at Selwood Academy in October 2018, where the meeting had taken place 60 years ago which led to the formation of the Society; this is described by Hilary Daniel in the Yearbook. The other was the sad occasion when Michael McGarvie, the most outstanding local historian of Frome, who has done so much for the Society, resigned as our President. I thank him for all that he has done for Frome and FSLS over more than 50 years.

Finally, I commend to you the new Yearbook; the back cover is inspirational, the work of well known and beloved local artist, Stina Falle. The Yearbook itself is, as usual, full of fascinating information about Frome, past and present. I am sure that you will enjoy it.

Sara Morris
Chairman

CONTENTS

The Elusive Louisa* Part I
by Suzanne Cooke

It all began with a phone call from my solicitor who was overseeing the purchase of my house in Frome. I had just moved from a 1960s open-plan house in Berkshire, with no history, to a three-storey late Victorian villa in Frome called Heatherlea. He sounded as excited as any solicitor ever gets when he told me delightedly that we had a full set of deeds plus some death certificates, for all the owners of Heatherlea, and that I might like to view them before he filed them away in the strongroom. They arrived a few days later, and as I unfolded the stiff paper of the earliest documents, the history of the house began to unfold.

It soon became apparent that the first owner, a certain Louisa Tuck, was of much greater interest to me than any of the other owners, such as the Spackmans who lived in the house from 1897 to 1936, the Long family, 1936-49 (Mr Long was a New Zealand farmer) or the Blairs (Mr Blair was a haulage contractor), and so my quest for Louisa began.

Heatherlea was built in 1893 by Sewards in Somerset Road overlooking Victoria Park which had been opened in 1887. It is of typical Victorian design, one of the block of six town houses, as we would call them now, stonebuilt with lots of decorative work on the front elevation and absolutely bland at the back. As I started to study the original documents more closely, I discovered that Louisa Tuck had moved from 28 Daneville Street, Camberwell, which was then part of Surrey, and that she had purchased the house newly built from the builders in November 1893 for the princely sum of £400. Checking my A-Z of London, I found a Daneville Road, SE 5, just off Peckham Road, so, believing that the Camberwell area of the 1890s was quite a select part of Surrey, I presumed that Louisa must have been a well-to-do woman. After all, the house she bought in Frome was expensive for that time and had many modern features: hot and cold water, inside toilet and electric bells, to name but a few.

Louisa only lived in the house for two years before she died in 1895, which means she does not appear in any census. Questions began to fill my mind: What brought her to Frome? How old was she when she died? What was the cause of her death? Where was she buried? Unfortunately, unlike some of the later occupants of Heatherlea, for whom there were death certificates, there was none for Louisa.

My search next took me to the local churchyard but I had no luck there, although I did find the gravestones of later occupants of the house. Then in July, I noticed that the Dissenters' Cemetery in Vallis Way was about to hold its yearly Open Day, when registers and maps of the site would be available for scrutiny.

*This article was first published in *Frome Hundred, Round Tower, 2004*

Heatherlea

Armed with pen and notebook along I went, however, before I had started checking names in registers and gravediggers' books, I noticed a headstone for a Stephen Tuck, who, I later discovered, wrote *The History of Methodism.* Could he be a link with my Louisa? I found that numerous Tucks were listed, but there was no Louisa. The only possibility was a Harriet Tuck (widow) of Somerset Road, died January 1895 aged 65. It was the right year and the right road: could this be Louisa? I came away confused.

I was soon to discover that the house was auctioned off after her death, but, a further mystery, why did it take from January to May before the auction was held? Contents included a piano, walnut furniture, a sewing machine, French metal bedstead (so much easier to control the bedbugs), jewel boxes and oddly, two clothes posts and wire line. Queen Victoria was still on the throne, Gladstone was Prime Minister, and women were beginning to have lives of their own, especially if they had money (although they were still a long way from having the vote). It would have been unusual but not remarkable, for a woman on her own, to move from one side of the country to the other and set up house; but still what had brought her to Frome? Did she come alone? Perhaps she brought a maid with her; after all, the house had electric bells in each room, or had she a companion or relative living with her? There would certainly have been enough room, with five bedrooms and a boxroom.

By this time various friends had realised my interest in Louisa and offered to do some searching on my behalf. One looked up 'Tuck' on different websites for tracing family history, but nothing concrete came of it: just more lists and queries. Another friend even suggested that Miss or Mrs Tuck (both titles are used in the official documents) was some gentleman's fancy woman and that he had purchased Heatherlea to be near him in his country mansion. After all this was the era of Alice Keppel, mistress of the Prince of Wales, and *Mrs Warren's Profession* by George Bernard Shaw had been written but was banned until 1902.

My next port of call was Frome Museum, where I searched endlessly through the somewhat chaotic filing system but to no avail. I did find mention of a John Tuck of Badcox Lane Baptist Church: Mr Tuck was a bookseller[1], father to the present Miss Tuck of Zion Chapel. They were originally Wesleyan and he was a very acceptable local preacher and sometimes supplied other pulpits in the town.[2] Another religious link perhaps? Did Louisa move down here after she was widowed to be near her relatives? But if so, and she was using her married name, pursuing Tucks through records and gravestones would not help, unless she moved to be near her in-laws. If so, what I needed was her maiden name.

My next visit was to Ames Kent, the solicitors, still in Frome, who had dealt with the auction and sale of the house after Louisa died. Yet again it was a dead end, literally, as they do not keep wills and related documents for that far back. So where did the money from the sale of the house go, and why, if Louisa moved to be near her relatives, didn't they get the furniture?

Another afternoon was spent at Frome Library searching through the Somerset Standard on microfiche for the announcement of Louisa's death. Nothing showed up for her death, but I did find a report of the auction sale.

Visualise a sunny day in May 1895:

'Property sale. On Thursday afternoon quite an innovation occurred, viz a sale by auction of a house on the premises. In the presence of a large company assembled on the lawn in the rear of Heatherlea, Somerset Road, and in brilliant sunshine, Messrs Harding and Son sold the freehold of recently erected residence and garden, which after good competition was bought by Mr ER Trotman* at £390 besides £10.10s. for fixtures. A detached kitchen garden of 20 perches was bought by the same purchaser for £41. Messrs EG Ames and Son were the vendor's solicitors. After the sale of the property the furniture was disposed of at good prices.'

In the deeds is a copy of the auction details plus a list of the furniture and effects. With this information, I am able to conjure up a picture of Louisa, but not how old she is. As I sit in my lounge, I can visualise her sitting on her couch, made of walnut and upholstered in figured damask, gazing into the painted slate fireplace with brass fire curb and set of fire brasses, or perhaps playing a waltz on her cottage piano, then possibly sleeping in her 4'6'' brass-mounted iron French bedstead with wire mattress, surrounded by her pine bedroom suite including marble top washstand or bathing in the roll-top ball and clawfoot enamelled bath; or walking in the small garden checking the cucumber frame next to the 60 gallon iron tank.

It is all too easy to visualise, but who was Louisa and why did she come to Frome? What caused her death, and where is she buried? Maybe one day I shall discover the truth about the elusive Louisa; I hope so.

[1] *FSLS Yearbook 14, 2011*
[2] *Edward Trotman letter, Frome Museum library D526*

The Trotmans are a mystery in themselves: was Edward Trotman, the writer of the letter, the ER Trotman who bought Louisa's house? What relation was Edward Vaughan Trotman, who had bought the house next door in 1893?

Suzanne Cooke carried out her research in 2002; it was only in 2018 that John Millns discovered the answer to her questions which he describes in Part II. Ed

The Elusive Louisa Part II
by John Millns

Since finding a second-hand copy of *Frome Hundred* last summer and reading Suzanne Cooke's captivating short story *The Elusive Louisa*, I had been wondering whether she had discovered why Louisa Tuck had apparently returned to Frome from Camberwell in 1893. How fortunate to learn Suzanne was still hoping to hear more about Louisa one day. So, who was Louisa?

Louisa was the fifth generation of Tucks to live in Frome.[1] Her father, Edwin Tuck (1823-1888) was an accomplished artisan in the town working as a cordwainer. After marrying a local girl, Harriet Starr in 1850, followed by several years living and working in Clerkenwell EC1 as a master shoemaker, Edwin and his young family returned to live in Frome shortly before the birth of their third child, Louisa.

BAPTISMS solemnized in the Parish of *The Holy Trinity Frome* in the County of *Somerset* in the Year 18 *50*						
When Baptized.	Child's Christian Name.	Parents' Name. Christian.	Surname.	Abode.	Quality, Trade, or Profession.	By whom the Ceremony was performed.
18*50.* Feb 7th	Louisa	Edwin and Harriett	Tuck	Union St.	Cordwain	A Daniel
No. 481						

Louisa Tuck was baptised at Holy Trinity, Frome on 7 February 1858

Louisa was born on 1 December 1857 and baptised the following February at Holy Trinity Church, built to serve the local working community in 1838. The family were living off Vallis Way at 19 Union Street,[1] a terraced cottage backing onto Edward Trotman's Badcox Brewery opened in 1848. By 1861 Edwin and Harriet had a growing family to clothe and feed; their eldest child Henry was 9, Charles 5, Louisa 3 and her brother Alfred just 1-year-old.[2]

As the granddaughter of John Tuck (c1785-1829), bookbinder, lay preacher and Trustee at the Baptist Chapel in Badcox Lane,[1] Louisa shared some of the qualities of her aunts Caroline and Arabella, well-connected, educated and independent daughters of her grandfather's younger brother Stephen Tuck (1792-1865), printer and author of the book *Wesleyan Methodism in Frome*. During the 1850s and 1860s, Caroline and Arabella ran a private boarding 'establishment for young ladies' known as the 'Ladies Seminary' at their father's three-storey house at 11 Keyford Terrace,[2] one of a fine terrace of fourteen houses behind the old Butts Hill Iron Works. As many of Louisa's relatives had long left

Frome to live and work in Shoreditch and Clerkenwell in London EC1, her spinster aunts Caroline and Arabella would have been a natural choice as Louisa's God mothers in Frome.

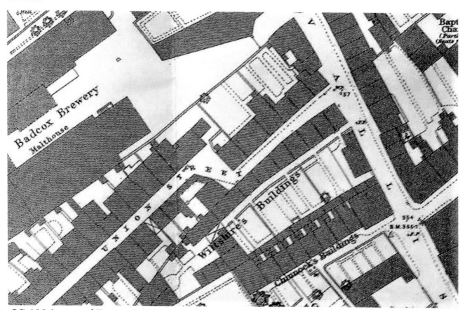

OS 1886 map of Frome 1:500 scale showing Badcox Brewery, Union Street and Wiltshires Buildings

*Wiltshires Buildings in the 1950s
Photo: Frome Museum*

By 1871, Louisa's parents had moved with their seven children from Union Street to larger accommodation in nearby 6 Wiltshires Buildings,[1] a terrace of two and three storey houses accessed by footpath from Vallis Way. Louisa's eldest brother Henry 19 was working as a house painter, Charles 16 a carpenter, Alfred 11, Emma 8 and Joseph 6 were still at school and Frederick was 1-year-old.[2] However, on the night of the census, 13-year-old Louisa was not at home because she was a boarding pupil at the charity asylum for girls at Culverhill on the edge of the rural hamlet of Lower Keyford.[2]

Louisa was one of 21 girl scholars between the ages of 11 and 17 boarding in Stevens' Asylum,[2] an educational foundation for local girls from 'poor' families. The scholars had been elected by the church elders in the parish for further education and training for domestic service at this

9

exceptional school funded by Richard Stevens' charity where 'they also attended prayers every morning and evening in the chapel, except on Sundays when they went to church with the matron'.[3]

Stevens' Asylum and Hospital in Culverhill engraved by Joseph Lambert in 1805
Photo: Images of Frome

Charity girls wearing their ankle-length gowns and distinctive bonnets by the east wall of the Blue House originally came from the Asylum's façade at Culverhill

The Asylum not only provided free boarding for girls but also incorporated a free 'hospital' or refuge for about ten old men, mostly widowers, from the local community.[3]

By 1881, Louisa's older brothers, Henry and Charles, had left Frome for Clerkenwell and joined their father's brother and three sisters who had left Frome in the 1840s before the brothers moved to Camberwell. Meanwhile, Louisa and sister Emma were living 150 miles away in the small village of Ashley in Staffordshire, both in domestic service to Stirling Voules, Rector of Ashley, with his wife Isabella and 5-year-old daughter. The sisters may well have been in Ashley for several years.

10

Louisa, now 23 was employed as nurse and domestic servant with her 18-year-old sister Emma serving the family as the housemaid.[2]

Three years later, Louisa was back in Frome briefly to attend and witness Emma's marriage to William Francis Woodland, at Holy Trinity in December 1884; [2] a little later, Emma moved with her husband to Maidstone.

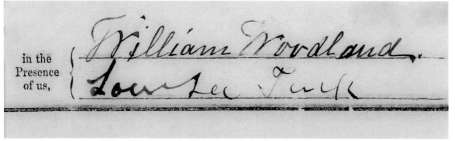

Marriage witnessed by the groom's father and the bride's sister Louisa Tuck

Louisa's father Edwin died in 1888 aged 66. Like many of the Tucks of his generation, he was buried in the non-conformists' Vallis Road cemetery in Frome which left his widow at home in Wiltshires Buildings with only her youngest 18-year-old son still at home.[2]

With Louisa's two elder brothers now living in Camberwell and her sister Emma in Maidstone, it was likely that one day Louisa would move to south London. Emma's widowed mother was also staying in Maidstone with her daughter's family in 1891while

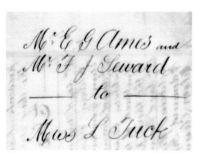

Conveyance and Title Deeds dated 9th November 1893

Louisa was employed as the residential housekeeper to a wealthy commercial traveller and widower with his nineteen-year-old student son living at 156 Denmark Hill,[2] a substantial detached villa opposite Ruskin Park, just a few minutes' walk from Louisa's brothers Henry and Charles. Within two years, Louisa was living in a three-storey terraced property with a basement half a mile away in Daneville Street.[6]

In Part I, Suzanne Cooke describes how it was Miss Louisa Tuck who purchased *Heatherlea* in Somerset Road in 1893. The new house was one of a 'rank' of six three-storey late Victorian terraced villas built by FJ Seward and Sons of Butts Hill* on 'a close of pasture land situated on the east side of a lane leading from the Butts to the Union Workhouse'.[6]

Seward FJ, Sewards of Frome, FSLS Yearbook 5, 1993-4

The villa was complete with five bedrooms and looked onto the newly laid out recreation ground, Victoria Park. The *Title Deeds* of 9 November 1893 confirmed the property was conveyed to 'Louisa Tuck of 28 Daneville Street, Camberwell in the County of Surrey, Spinster, for the price of £400.' So how did Louisa raise such a large sum?

Louisa was well educated, she could read and write, unlike many of her mother's generation, and highly practised in domestic services. She would have earned a good salary of up to £60 per year. What is certain is that Louisa Tuck somehow acquired *Heatherlea* with her name on the *Title Deeds* and on completion paid £400 to EG Ames the local solicitors. But was this sum from her own savings?

It wasn't Louisa Tuck who unexpectedly died fourteen months later in January 1895; Louisa was very much alive, still single and with many years' professional housekeeping and nursing experience for the wealthy middle-class. The death that year in *Heatherlea* was that of Louisa's widowed mother, 65-year-old Harriet!

So, could the reason for Louisa's apparent return to Frome from Camberwell have been to care for her ageing mother Harriet and run the household? If this was the explanation, then it is reasonable to think a family 'collection plate' may have been passed around Louisa's siblings to help towards the villa's purchase.

Following Harriet's death so soon after moving into Somerset Road and apparently before making her Will,[5] Louisa would have needed a *Letter of Attorney* in order to finalise her mother's affairs. As the lawfully confirmed family representative of the late Mrs Tuck,[7] Louisa appointed local solicitors EG Ames and Son of Cork Street to act as her agents who instructed auctioneers Harding and Sons of King Street to sell the following lots by auction on 16th May 1895.

Dated. *16th May 1895*

Miss Tuck's Sale

LOT 1.

The sale of the newly built freehold Villa in Somerset Road

Lot 1 Villa   £390
Fixtures and fittings   £10.10s

Lot 2 Kitchen Garden   £41

The kitchen garden or nursery was an additional sizeable plot of land which had been conveyed to Louisa on 10 July 1894. The total realised from the auction of Lots 1 and 2 was £441. 10s. with an additional auctioneer's fee of £9. Immediately following the auction, Mrs Tuck's collection of modern furniture was also auctioned.[7]

The highest bidder for the villa and kitchen garden on the day of the auction was Edward R Trotman of Frome United Breweries, who immediately transferred both Lots to Mr Charles H Spackman in consideration of the sum of £19. 10s.[7] In other words, Edward Trotman was paid a fee to bid at the auction on behalf of the Spackmans. It was 33-year-old Charles Spackman, a solicitor's clerk and his wife who became the new owners of *Heatherlea* and not Trotman. Charles needed a bidder if he worked as the legal clerk to the vendor's solicitor and knew the vendor!

During his childhood, Charles Spackman had lived with his parents at 8 Keyford Terrace, just three doors away from the Tuck sisters which suggests a life-time link between Charles, Louisa and her aunts Caroline and Arabella. Following completion of the purchase on 24 June 1895,[7] Charles, his wife Ellinor and Reginald their new born son moved into *Heatherlea*.[2] The Spackmans stayed for many years next door to Edward Vaughan Trotman and his family; he was the son of ER Trotman.

At the time of the auction in May, the villa's *Annexed Particulars* attached to the *Conditions of Sale and Contract* confirmed that the Auctioneers were 'favoured with instructions from Representatives of the late Mrs Tuck' to sell by auction the freehold villa, kitchen garden and furniture. Could this mean that Louisa was not the rightful owner after all?

At the time of the first purchase in 1893, Louisa may have used the *Letter of Attorney* giving her authorisation to act on behalf of her mother's private affairs. If so, then the £400 for the purchase would not have come from Louisa's savings but from the life-time savings of her mother Harriet. Therefore, the unexpected sale of *Heatherlea* in 1895 was, as the details in the *Annexed Particulars* went on to clarify, 'solely in consequence of the death of the late owner.' Mrs Tuck!

Louisa, still only 37, single and close to her brothers Henry and Charles, apparently returned to Camberwell SE5 in the summer of 1895. Before long, Louisa met a young man, Ernest Edward Constable, a farmer's son from nearby Court Farm in Court Lane, Dulwich in Camberwell and they married in 1900.[4] Two years after her marriage at the age of 42, Louisa Constable gave birth to Ernest's daughter Edna Elizabeth in 1902 in West Sussex, where they farmed the one-hundred-acre Black Hill Farm in Colgate on the edge of the ancient St Leonard's Forest near Horsham.[4]

NAME AND SURNAME	RELATIONSHIP to Head of Family.	AGE (last Birthday) and SEX.		PARTICULARS as to MARRIAGE.					PROFESSION of Persons aged
1.	2.	Ages of Males.	Ages of Females.	5.	6.	7.	8.	9.	10.
1 Ernest Constable	Head	39		Married					Farmer	100
2 Louisa Constable	Wife		45	Married	10	1	1		
3 Edna Constable	Daughter	7	7	Single					

(To be filled up by, or on behalf of, the Head of Family or other person in occupation, or in charge, of this dwelling.)

Write below the Number of Rooms in this Dwelling (House, Tenement, or Apartment). Count the kitchen as a room but do not count scullery, landing, lobby, closet, bathroom; nor warehouse, office, shop.

7

I declare that this Schedule is correctly filled up to the best of my knowledge and belief.

Signature *Ernest E. Constable*

Postal Address *Blue Hill. Colgate. Horsham. Sussex*

Ernest gave Louisa's age incorrectly in the April 1911 Census. Louisa was 53-years-old

Sometime before 1939 and the outbreak of WWII, Louisa and Ernest retired to 20 Heathfield Road, a large late Victorian villa in South Croydon.[4] During the 1940-41 'Blitz,' the neighbourhood was hit with heavy bombing and after a period of 'incapacitation' while working as a volunteer Air Raid Precautions (ARP) Warden, Louisa died in 1943 at the age of 85 leaving the substantial sum of £4,347 to her husband Ernest and daughter Edna.[5] She was buried in Camberwell cemetery where her husband was buried in 1960, leaving an estate of £24,241.[5]

Surprisingly, Louisa was thirteen years Ernest's senior, many more than had been acknowledged in census returns according to her date of birth given on the 1939 electoral roll as 1 December 1869, the same day Louisa had celebrated her twelfth birthday with school friends back at Stevens' Asylum for girls in Culverhill!

[1] https://www.wikitree.com/genealogy/Tuck-Family-Tree-66
[2] *Ancestry UK Census, Baptism, Marriage and Burial Records*
[3] *History and Description of Public Charities in the Town of Frome, Penny, 1833*
[4] *Ray Tuck, private communication*
[5] https://probatesearch.service.gov.uk/
[6] *Conveyance and Title Deeds for* Heatherlea, *1893*
[7] *Particulars and Conditions of Sale and Contract, 1895*

My thanks to Suzanne Cooke for sharing her earlier research and original documents which helped to unlock the second part of this mystery, also, many thanks to Frome Research and Frome Hundred groups, Ray Tuck and to Frome Museum.

Saving Marston House
by Michael McGarvie

Once again the threat of destruction looms over Marston House. Soon Somerset County Council is to consider another proposal to pull it down. It is a good moment to pause and consider; it is astonishing that a house of this quality and the seat of such a well-known family as that as the earls of Cork and Orrery should have been so little studied. Until now no one has written its history or studied its architecture. The meagre items which have appeared in print about Marston House have been superficial and ill-informed. Thanks largely to the investigations undertaken by the Frome Society for Local Study, there is a growing awareness that a house of great architectural and historical value is at risk. This knowledge has been disseminated widely and if the house is now destroyed, it will be by those who were aware of the facts, but chose to ignore them. It can only represent a triumph of vandalism over civilisation.

We cannot be certain of the origins of Marston House, but it is likely that the first house on this site was built by Sir Thomas Vavasour, who was Knight Marshal to James I, about 1610. Vavasour also owned Ham House, near Petersham in Surrey, which was designed for him by John Smithson, a well-known Jacobean architect. In old prints showing the two houses before they were altered, they are remarkably alike and this makes it probable that Smithson was also the architect of Marston. His work is represented today by the central block with its double recessed front, basically unchanged, and a variation of the H-shaped houses of the Elizabethans. In 1638, the Great Earl of Cork bought the house and described it in a letter to his steward as 'fair' and possessing 'orchards, gardens and pleasant walks about it.' He held court there on 8 October 1641 before going on to Frome to hold an attornment, a ceremony at which the tenants acknowledged him as their landlord. After his death in 1643 the property was inherited by his youngest son, Roger, Lord Broghill, afterwards first Earl of Orrery.

It was at this time that Robert Boyle, the famous philosopher and scientist, lived in the house and a letter exists from him to an unknown lady, dated from Marston on 26 March 1649. From this year too, dates the story of Lord Broghill's encounter with Rev Mr Asberry. One day when Lord Broghill was attending Marston Church and had heard a dull discourse from a Puritan divine, an unknown person offered to preach and did so excellently. Broghill invited him to dinner and he proved to be a Church of England clergyman named Asberry, who had been ejected by the Puritans. He told his host 'I have lived three years in a poor cottage under your warren wall... my son lives with me and we dig and read by turns. I have a little money and some few books, and I submit cheerfully to the will of providence.' Such homeless clergy must have been common at the time, but Asberry's story made an extraordinary impression on Broghill, and on his descendants. Broghill secured him a pension of £30 a year, a comfortable income, and he and his son, Charles, were painted, portraits which remained at Marston until 1905. Later a rustic cottage was built to commemorate the episode, but has since disappeared.

The year 1711 was important in the history of Marston. In that year, Charles, fourth Earl of Orrery, diplomat, soldier and man of letters or, as the *Gentleman's Magazine* summed it up, a great virtuoso, was created an English baron, as Irish titles carried no seat in the House of Lords. So, a remote and scattered Somerset village became the *caput baroniae* of the Barony of Boyle of Marston. The house was then very neglected and the new baron, as his son tells us, 'added a wing to complete the fabric and by that means has enlarged the house and rendered the building uniform and regular without.' Yet when he died in 1731, Marston was still as his daughter-in-law was to record, 'much out of repair without offices or stables, little more than the shell of a large old house.' Her husband, John, the fifth Earl of Orrery, *litterateur* and friend of the leading literary lights of the day, restored the house, building the stables and coach houses, and 'fitting up and furnishing different apartments.' Lady Orrery tells us that 'the hours he was not employed in his studies he amused himself in laying out gardens and other plantations.' To do this he employed Stephen Switzer, a Hampshire man of Swiss origin, who was proud of his work at Marston. A print exists which shows the gardens as he left them, sweeping down the hillside, in front of the house, a formal arrangement of walls, steps and pools.

Having beautified the grounds and having dotted them with memorials to his horse, King Nobby, and to his dog, Hector, Lord Orrery could no longer tolerate the old-fashioned

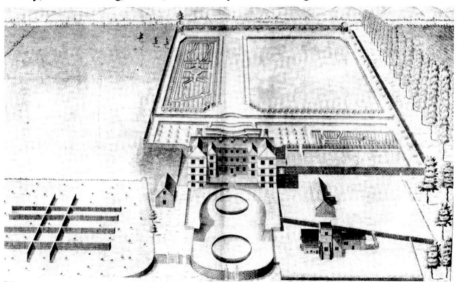

Marston House and gardens as they were in 1739

appearance of Marston House and between 1749 and 1752 he remodelled it to create the appearance of a fashionable Palladian mansion. The date 1751 is on the rainwater heads but Lady Orrery also recorded that her husband 'had taken off the roof, very much adorned the outside, put in new windows and window cases, built a new staircase and made great alterations on the inside.' Basically, the work consisted of replacing the high-pitched roofs with mansards, adding the elegant balustrade and dentilled cornice round the top of the building, and replacing the transom windows with sashes surrounded by stone mouldings and voussoir blocks.

In his *Remarks on Swift*, Lord Orrery tells us of his pleasure 'in viewing a plain regular building composed by a masterly hand in all the beauty of symmetry and order.' Perhaps he was thinking of Marston when he wrote, for he describes his own work admirably. The facade is exquisite and worthy of preservation in its own right. One would give much to know the architect. It might be the work of Nathaniel Ireson of Wincanton, or, if we are to believe Lady Orrery, her eldest son, Lord Dungarvan, 'whose genius is very much inclined towards architecture,' was responsible.

A hereditary gout carried Orrery, now also Earl of Cork, off from 'this dear and delightful place' in 1762 and his son and successor died two years later at the age of 35. The funeral cost the Frome churchwardens 6s paid to four men for keeping off the mob. His brother Edmund inherited Marston and soon found that, despite his father's improvements, the house was too small. He therefore added two long, low wings in the Adam style which, although they lack the quality of the central facade, are simple nicely balanced compositions. Earl Edmund also removed the church from its position in front of the house to the side, no doubt to improve the view, and add to his privacy; this was in 1786. During his last years, the seventh Earl, who was Colonel of the Somerset Regiment of militia, spent most of his time in Bath leading a voluptuous life and hardly had his son, another Edmund succeeded him in 1798, when he put in hand what the Rev Richard Warner called 'judicious alterations.' These were designed not only to 'improve the mansion without, but render it much more comfortable within....and the house altogether be made more secluded, quiet and retired, by turning the public road which runs along the front.' The closure of the road (it is still a right of way) allowed for further improvements, the most definite of which was the removal of the main entrance from the south to the north front. The basement storey on the south was now buried to make way for a stately terrace which occupies the whole length of the south front. The old front door was removed to make way for a charming one-storey Ionic portico whose taste was influenced by the Greek revival. This is of exceptional quality and may be the work of Sir Jeffrey Wyattville, famous for his rebuilding of Windsor Castle, whose noble profile we owe to him. Wyattville included Lord Cork among his patrons and there are references to his going to Lord Cork's and to Lord Cork visiting him in the years 1817 and 1819. We know that the portico was finished by 1822 when Neale drew the house. No doubt it it was at this time that Lord Orrery's gardens were swept away without trace in favour of a more natural landscape and Wyattville would have been just the man to do it.

It was left to the ninth Earl in 1858, to add Marston's most grandiose feature, a new entrance hall on the north front. 'It is' wrote Samuel Cuzner in 1867, 'a commanding and handsome stone structure, of the classic order of architecture. Its exterior embellishments, in stone carving, as well as the massive doorway, are imposing and elegant. The interior of the hall is grand striking in effect, not only from its lofty and spacious dimensions, but also from the lantern light at the top.'

Marston House: drawing by Neale 1822

A grand staircase was erected at the same time and led up to additional suites of rooms. The designs were by Major CE Davis, the City Architect of Bath. The entrance hall was admirably executed and some authorities believe it to be the finest feature of the house. The Victorian Society is strongly opposed to its demolition.   Enough has been said to show that Marston is not some mediocre country house, but a building of great interest and merit whose quality is becoming increasingly recognised. It is extremely fortunate that this knowledge has come to light in the nick of time. That a mansion of this size and calibre has previously gone by default is a reflection on the methods of investigation of the Government department concerned.

We must not overlook the landscape and amenity value of Marston House. Everyone who knows it will be aware of the superb position it occupies above the Vale of Witham. One glance at the house across the valley will carry instant conviction of its landscape value. The view across the vale from the Wiltshire ridge was described by the historian Collinson as 'the most beautiful inland prospect in the kingdom.' This view still remains, perhaps now even richer and more diversified. Marston House is an integral part of this view and an essential ingredient. For its architecture, for its history, for its associations, for its place in the landscape, Marston House must be saved.

Michael McGarvie's research as shown in this article, published in the Somerset Standard on 8 June 1973, was critical in saving Marston House from demolition. Ed

From the Trinity Area to Bristol
Town houses further explored
By Roger Leech

From my own experience as an archaeologist studying buildings I see no divide between two disciplines called history and archaeology. Another now widely recognised branch of archaeology is historical archaeology part of which I would see as concerned with the archaeology of buildings. The historical archaeologist studying buildings will work as an architectural historian placing buildings in their physical and topographical contexts, within their own craft and design tradition, but also in their wider political and social context. I can best resort to demonstrating that this is so by reference to two projects in which I have been personally involved : Frome and Bristol.

The first of these studies was of early industrial housing in Frome[1]. In 1974, together with Professor Mick Aston, then County Archaeologist for Somerset, I was responsible for the production of a study of the archaeological implications of future development in the historic towns of Somerset. Mick was to study the towns in the west of the county, I those in the east. It was our practice to perambulate each town to be studied and one day in 1974 we looked at Frome.

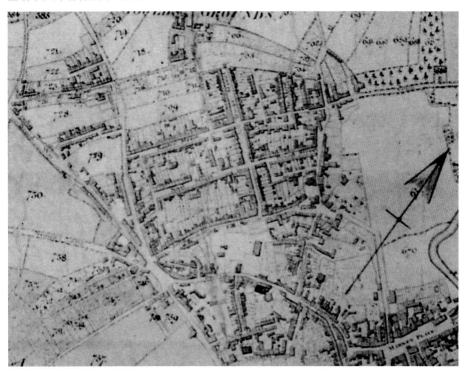

The north-west side of Frome on the 1813 map by Cruse

On the north-west side of the town the early 19th century map showed a regular suburb which we took first to be probably a Victorian suburb added to the earlier town. Walking down these streets we rapidly realised that they were lined by houses of the 17th century, largely refronted in the 19th century. Pinned to the doors of many of the houses were compulsory purchase orders presaging their planned demolition. Our response to this situation was rapid. The Regional Archaeological Unit, the Committee for Rescue Archaeology in Avon, Gloucestershire and Somerset (CRAAGS) took on the archaeological survey of the entire area to be demolished as a project, with funding from the Royal Commission on the Historical Monuments of England.

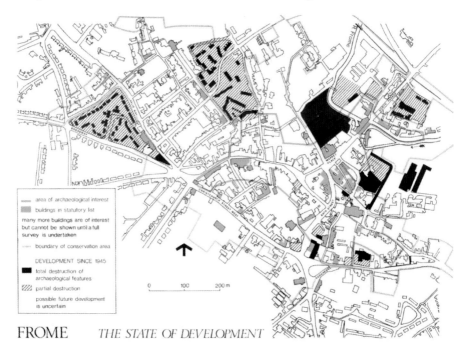

FROME   *THE STATE OF DEVELOPMENT*

The freshly completed new list of buildings of historic interest, which had inexplicably omitted a hundred or more surviving 17th century houses scheduled for demolition by the local authority, was rapidly revised by Francis Kelly, following a letter from a DoE official expressing some irritation. Following a feasibility study by Moxley Jenner and Partners of Bristol, the decision was then made that the 17th century suburb would be retained with the houses modernised to serve as new local authority housing. The restored housing was then given a ministerial re-opening, with William Waldegrave being presented with a copy of the RCHME published survey of the 17th century houses only recently scheduled for demolition and now listed as being of historic interest.

William Waldegrave (right) being presented with a copy of the RCHME survey

Early Industrial Housing, The Trinity Area of Frome[1] was based on what might be called an archaeologically informed survey. Buildings were placed in their physical and topographical contexts: the development of the street plan was traced through time, in c1665, c1685, c1705 and c1725; the building process was mapped in topographical context for five of the streets; the distribution of plan types was mapped across the area studied. The classification of plan types owed its inspiration to the then recently published study of vernacular housing in Wales.

The use of air photographs, normal for archaeological survey, was innovative in the area survey of a historic housing development. Here it enabled the identification retrospectively of the characteristics and plan forms of buildings in the half of the Trinity Area demolished in the 1960s Also normal for archaeological survey was the preparation of new plans of the structures within the study area. These revealed many of the complexities in the relationships between adjoining houses, contributing further to understanding of the building process.

Late 17th century buildings in Naish's Street, 1975. The houses on the left have been raised and re-fronted in the 19th century.

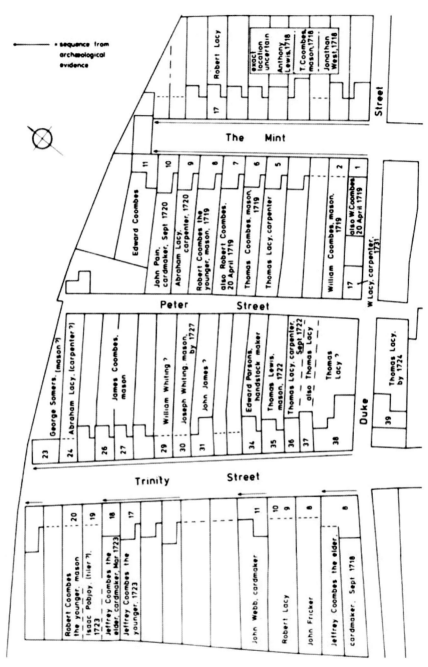

An extract from Early Industrial Housing, The Trinity Area of Frome[1], showing an analysis of Builders, Occupations and Dates.

The archaeological research was fully complemented by research based on documentary sources, from the Public, Somerset and Wiltshire Record Offices, from the local authorities for the properties which they now owned, and from some private sources. These provided a historical context to the building process and enabled the identification in the Public Record Office of the only probate inventory surviving for any of the houses, all others having been destroyed in the wartime bombing of the Devon Record Office in Exeter.

The second study, looking at buildings archaeology, was of the town house in medieval and early modern Bristol, which had its origins in a research project commenced in the late 1970s, inspired by work undertaken for the predecessors of English Heritage in evaluating the urban archaeological resource in the counties of Avon, Gloucestershire and Somerset. One particular outcome of this work was a study of 17th century housing in the town of Frome, the research for which revealed that, in looking for comparative material, almost nothing was available in print to understand the form and character of housing of the same period in Bristol, a city of major importance in the 17th century and but a short distance from Frome. In looking at this vacuum of knowledge it rapidly became evident that a considerable number of houses of the 17th century or earlier survived within Bristol, alongside a potentially vast quantity of relevant documentary material, plans, photographs, paintings and drawings.

Over the next 30 or more years I worked on this as a research project. Published in 2014, *The Town House in Medieval and Early Modern Bristol*[2] avoided a rigidly chronological analysis which would have taken in turn medieval, early post-medieval and 'Georgian' periods for successive treatment. The main chapters are instead focused on contemporary perceptions of the types of houses in which people lived, perceptions which can be related to the economic and social life of the city. In 1473 a clerk of Canynges' chantry in St Mary Redcliff in Bristol compiled an unusually detailed rental of the chantry's endowments. Individual properties were described in detail and within these descriptions a distinction was made between 'hallhouses' and 'shophouses'.

Several large medieval hallhouses can be identified and directly linked to social ascent and changing fortunes. In the 14th and 15th centuries members of the Canynges family emerged from comparative obscurity to become one of the city's wealthiest merchant dynasties. The elaborate open hall of Canynges' house in Redcliff Street reflected the wealth of this family in the 14th or early 15th centuries, but by the later 15th century it had become no more than the entrance to the courtyards and larger house beyond: a hall in the modern sense of being an entry passage. A second such house, much discussed in the book, was no. 20 Small Street, purchased at the Dissolution by John Smyth, a merchant whose family origins are, like those of the Canynges, clouded in obscurity. A new chamber block and the re-roofing of the open hall in the style of the new hammerbeam roof at Hampton Court, were additions of the mid-16th century, through which Smyth possibly celebrated and asserted his wealth and new purchases from the Crown. A century later, Small Street remained a location in which new wealth could assert its status in society and the militia. The Creswicks were the new residents of what had been Smyth's house at no.20, fit now in the first Civil War siege of Bristol in 1643 to receive an embattled king and his sons.

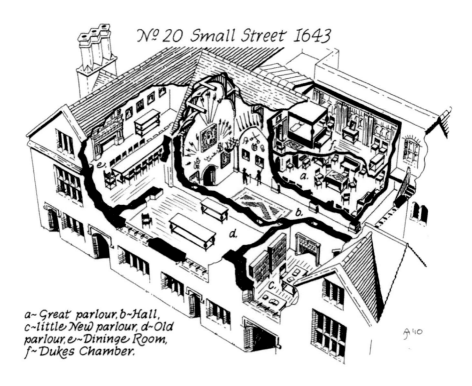

№ 20 Small Street 1643

a~ Great parlour, b~Hall,
c~little New parlour, d~Old
parlour, e~Dininge Room,
f~Dukes Chamber.

The form of the hallhouse could also be used for a tavern. The shophouse was identifiable from the unheated shop on the ground floor and living accommodation placed in the rooms above. No.43 Broad Street, built c1411, was one such shophouse, and remains the earliest surviving house in Bristol. Typical of shophouses in other medieval towns, it was built without any chimneystack and fireplace to provide for heating and cooking; the occupants of such houses would have resorted to taverns or their beds for warmth and to cook shops, medieval takeaways, for cooked food. Another such shophouse was no.31 High Street, described in the builder's contract of 1473 as having a shop on the ground floor, a hall over, and chambers above.

The terms 'hallhouse' and 'shophouse' possibly encapsulated a distinction between houses with an open hall and houses where the hall was a ceiled room over a ground-floor shop. This might have equated for the most part to a distinction between larger and smaller houses, between those of rich and less wealthy townspeople. What was significant about the distribution of these types of houses in Bristol is that, while some central streets were clearly the most prestigious residential areas, there is little sign in the Middle Ages of a strict social segregation: rich and poor still appear to have lived in close proximity.

The evidence from Bristol has pointed to this proximity disappearing from the later 17th and early 18th century, with the development of suburbs that were increasingly differentiated socially. Different house types cannot be correlated absolutely with social status, at least from the 17th century. Some shophouses close to the quaysides could be quite grand dwellings, suitable as residences for the urban elite. Shophouses existed in many cities and towns: London, Exeter, Salisbury and Ludlow, for example.

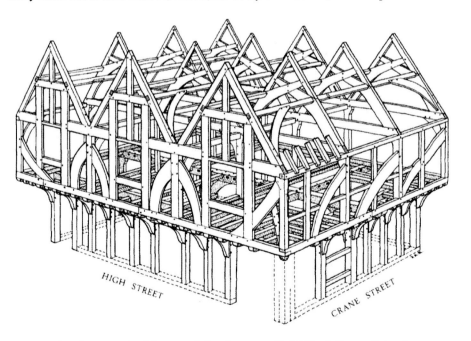

The timber framework of the grand shophouse at 52-54 High Street, Bristol

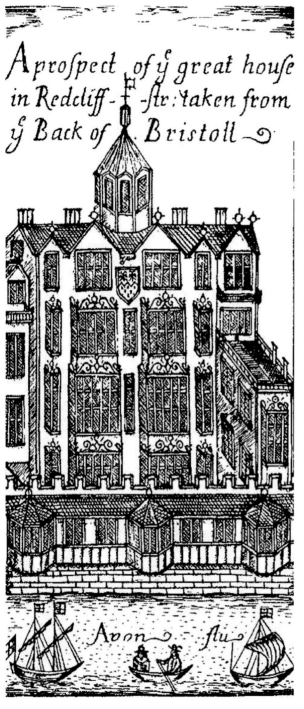

A prospect of ÿ great houſe in Redcliff-ſtr:taken from ÿ Back of Briſtoll

Avon flu

The residential house, most frequently of two rooms in depth with the stairs linking the separate floors, was based on that of the storeyed, late medieval shophouse. The building of these houses in such large numbers from the 1650s onwards transformed the appearance and fabric of Bristol, to the extent that by the end of the 18th century a large part of the population must have lived in what we might term two-parlour, storeyed residential houses. The town house played a critical role in affirming the position of the merchant elite in the medieval and early modern town and city. In the medieval period, and extending nearly to the end of the 17th century, larger hallhouses and particularly those fronting courtyards provided a means of displaying both wealth and status. Larger storeyed residential houses fulfilled the same role from the late 16th century onwards, the earliest of these being the great houses at the south end of Bristol Bridge on Redcliff Back and on St Augustine's Back. The construction of many hundreds of large and smaller storeyed residential houses in the 17th and 18th centuries formed a fundamental part of the process of creating a city with distinct residential neighbourhoods: the smallest of these were the equivalents of the rows of small houses recorded in the streets of the Trinity area in Frome.

The 1473 rental also described one house as a 'lodge'. A major feature in the later medieval and early modern townscape was the encirclement of the city with the second residences of the urban elite. From the evidence of houses, probate inventories and other documentary sources, it is clear that, in the 16th and 17th centuries, John Smyth of Small Street and Ashton Court, and Robert Cann of Corn Street and Stoke Bishop House, regarded themselves first as citizens of Bristol; but their descendants used the same country houses to project themselves as gentry. In the 18th century lodges were succeeded by garden houses, large numbers of which were built on the slopes of Clifton and Kingsdown.

The urban elite, not just merchants but others as well, thus created a distinct suburban landscape that has made a long lasting contribution to today's townscape. It might be seen as part of the order of merchant capitalism; also as possibly the inspiration for placing gardens to the front of rows of terraced houses, very much part of the design of the modern city.

By the 18th century, and to some extent from an earlier date, houses were almost without exception constructed to principles which possibly made hierarchy in society seem natural. Ground and first floors were areas for the display of wealth through panelling, plaster cornices, six panelled doors, open strings and hardwood handrails to the stairs. As one ascended through the house, panelling and plasterwork became increasingly absent. Doors were reduced first to four panels and then two, and the stairs to the uppermost storeys were given closed strings, a less expensive option than the alternative open string with the sides of the individual steps exposed to view. These variations were a means of economy, ways of making money go further. However, with reception rooms on the ground and first floors and servants' rooms on the upper floors, they also underlined cognitive links between expenditure, status and the design of the house. Such unwritten design principles were part of the early modern order of merchant capitalism.

74 Selwood Road, 1690s winder-stair with moulded risers

The 'Residential house', the house divorced from the place of work, is like the shophouse built on two or more floors, most often three. These were the houses of the Trinity area; how would one map the social and architectural topography of this area? At the house level, I would now look at finishes denoting hierarchy: stair finishes, door types, panels etc, for example, 74 Selwood Road.

Between houses, I would compare the plans mapped in 1981 in a slightly different way. Larger houses at corners were the houses of foremen and those occupying positions of responsibility in the nearby mills. I would need to know more of how the leasing of houses related to the workforce, and whose workforce it was. The leases are tabulated in the book[1] and lessees could be usefully linked to the lessors or mill proprietors.

Reconsidering this fascinating suburb of Frome we must be grateful for how much still survives and I would like to finish by underlining the contribution of your late member Derek Gill for all that he contributed to this and the study about which I have written in this article.

[1]*Leech RH, Early Industrial Housing, The Trinity Area of Frome, RCHM, 1981*
[2]*Leech RH, The Town House in Medieval and Early Modern Bristol, English Heritage, 2014*

This article is based on a lecture given to the Frome Society on 1 December 2018 by Roger Leech, Visiting Professor of Archaeology at the University of Southampton. Ed

The Trinity Area in 1925. This is the only photographic record of many of the houses since demolished.   *Reproduced courtesy of Aerofilms Ltd*

The Trinity Area: A Planning Timeline of its Conservation
by Bill Lowe

Introduction

In the beginning of the latter part of the 20th century, the reputation of Trinity was that of a slum because its building fabric had deteriorated to such an extent through a lack of inward investment by new households: Frome's population had declined in the early 20th century and thereafter had remained static whilst elsewhere in the country the population had seen significant growth.

1950s

Consequently, following the prevailing mood of the time, the former Frome Urban District Council (Frome UDC) decided that the whole of Trinity was "ripe for redevelopment", should be designated as a housing Clearance Area and that it should be successively redeveloped in stages (thereby unintentionally blighting the remainder and leading to a subsequent loss in community cohesion).

1960s

In 1960, the then Minister for Housing and Local Government (MHLG) approved a Compulsory Purchase Order (CPO) allowing the clearance of what became known as Trinity Phase 1, bounded by Selwood Road (to be realigned), Milk Street, Castle Street and Trinity Street. That clearance work was promptly completed and the area was rebuilt by 1967 to an unfortunate 1962 design by local architect Ronald Vallis. Redevelopment initially took the form of flats and houses to an unassuming geometric and utilitarian design with poor thermal performance. Fortunately for Trinity, this public housing stock has, in turn, been partly redeveloped in a more traditional manner and appearance, in the form that we now see it today.

A comprehensive statutory system of land use planning had been introduced in 1948 but it was not until 1960 that a diagrammatic Town Map for Frome was published as part of the Somerset County Development Plan 1958, and this was eventually approved by MHLG in 1965. This proposed a series of new roads to cut through the urban fabric with the objective of pedestrianising the town centre. For Trinity, a new link road from Badcox to Cork Street (the Sun Street link) was proposed, but only in diagrammatic form, promulgated so as to aid the rear servicing of Catherine Street and to create a more direct vehicular route to the town centre from A362 Radstock Road. The source of funding for this road was unclear (was it to be development led based on the broad zonings in the Town Map, or publicly funded?) Its detailed alignment, its proposed width and its junction details were yet to be finalised.

Following on from the eventual MHLG approval of the 1960 Town Map, in 1968 plans were laid before the MHLG for the clearance of Trinity Phase 2, bounded by Trinity

Street, a realigned Selwood Road, Dyer's Close Lane and Holy Trinity Churchyard. The north east side of Trinity Street was, however, to be retained and restored for use as elderly persons' accommodation.

1970s

In 1971, Frome UDC made the controversial no 5 Housing Compulsory Purchase Order covering the remaining Trinity 3 area extending from Vallis Road to Trinity Street. This was eventually confirmed in April 1974 by the newly created Department of the Environment (DoE, which replaced the MHLG). By 1972, Somerset's planning policy documents were looking increasingly out of date as a means of managing development, but the formal approval process was lengthy. So, the County Council published an updated but informal Town Plan for Frome which led to the development of the outlying Stonebridge area in the north of the town. Unfortunately for Trinity, this informal plan retained the Sun Street link, again without any mention of a funding stream. Opportunity purchases and compulsory acquisition of property within the putative road alignments and in Trinity 3 were being made by Somerset CC and Frome UDC after 1974 in furtherance of their plans.

In Trinity 3, there were 143 remaining houses, in the area bounded by Trinity Street, Selwood Road, Castle Street, Vallis Way and Orchard Street, but now this housing was belatedly becoming recognised in urban archaeological terms as having great heritage significance, compared to Frome UDC's earlier description of it as being 'ripe for redevelopment'. By the mid-1970s, that half of the housing stock which had been publicly acquired in Trinity 3 was empty and half of it was still privately owned and occupied, but severely blighted.

It was a piece of good fortune that Trinity 3 was left until last by Frome UDC; it is the oldest part of the area and is of the greatest heritage significance, having been recognised as the earliest remaining large area of industrial workers' housing in Britain, following on from research work by the Campaign for Rescue Archaeology in Avon, Gloucestershire and Somerset. Trinity 1 and 2, by contrast, had comprised largely 19th century housing of limited heritage significance.

The significance of the built fabric of Trinity 3 can be traced back to the restoration of the Monarchy in 1660, by which time confidence had returned to the Town's wool trade and the development of the Trinity 3 area started at its southern end, off the road to Radstock at Vallis Way. The earliest housing dates from the 1670s, initially laid out by Richard Yerbury for his workers in the wool trade. Frontage development along Castle Street then followed (named after a woman, not a fortress), with Trinity Street and outlying Milk Street later. Naish's Street was laid out in 1690 by John Selwood. William Whitchurch and his daughter Susannah developed the western end of Trinity Street which was completed in the early 18th century.

In the first half of the 1970s widespread public discontent with the housing clearances of the 1950s and 60s, with the consequent loss of community cohesion, had led to a reaction in favour of rehabilitation, not demolition and redevelopment; attitudes had also changed in professional planning practice. By now, in Trinity almost all of the Naish's Street housing was in public ownership along with parts of Trinity Street, Vallis Way, Baker Street, York Street and the northern part of Selwood Road in the historically significant Trinity 3 area.

On 1 April 1974 the reorganisation of local government took place and Frome UDC ceased to exist. Its housing and delegated planning function from Somerset County Council passed to the newly created Mendip District Council (Mendip); the housing function stayed in Frome at North Hill House, but the planning function was now based at Highfield House in Shepton Mallet. The opportunity and compulsory property purchases which had been made in Trinity 3 passed from Frome UDC to Mendip. Those within the assumed road alignment of the Sun Street link were owned by Somerset County Council as the highway authority.

As early as 1971 the Frome and District Civic Society had started to campaign for the retention and conservation of Trinity 3 in response to the making of the no 5 Housing Compulsory Purchase Order by Frome UDC. In May 1974, the Society produced its own plan for the rehabilitation of the area in which the work of local architect, the late Rodney Goodall, featured prominently. In response to the hostility generated by the recent confirmation of the latest CPO by the DoE, the "Save Trinity" campaign intensified.

By 1977, Mendip had established a team of specialist planning professionals in post under its Chief Planning Officer, Ray Bush and, with support from Somerset County Council's conservation planning team, declared all of the older parts of Frome as a Conservation Area, later to be classed as "outstanding" in the emerging Somerset County Structure Plan which was to replace the outdated County Development Plan of 1958, and which had been updated, but only informally, in 1972. This was despite the Sun Street link and other 1960s road proposals still being live projects for the traffic engineers in Somerset's Highways Department. The assumed road alignments were still being protected based on the diagrammatic proposals in the informal 1972 Town Plan. The blighting effect on the wider Trinity area therefore continued and private investment in the area suffered from a lack of confidence. However, Mendip's view of the future planning of Frome now was markedly different. Proposals for new roads, extra parking and pedestrianisation of the town centre were seen to be unduly optimistic, particularly in context of the financial constraints on local government brought about by the IMF crisis of 1976.

By March 1977, 82 of the houses were empty in Trinity 3 and in the wider area including the Sun Street link road area east of Castle Street, known locally as the Piggeries. A total of 87 houses had been acquired by local authority agreement or by compulsory purchase. The community spirit which had been prevalent in the area in the past had consequently been lost.

On 10 May 1977, in an attempt to resolve this impasse between conservation on the one hand and redevelopment on the other, Moxley, Jenner and Partners (MJP: a Bristol based practice of architects, planners, engineers and landscape architects) were instructed by Mendip to advise on the relative merits of rehabilitation or whether to continue with the redevelopment of Trinity 3. On 04 October 1977, their Report came down decisively in favour of rehabilitation as a comprehensive publicly funded exercise. Mendip subsequently resolved to retain its acquired properties and renovated housing in public ownership, rather than sell them on as recommended by MJP, to be kept as part of its social housing stock using central government loans and grant aid, despite the tighter funding constraints now in place. Those surviving houses which were still in private ownership were included in a broadly defined "General Improvement Area" extending from Gould's Ground in the west to Castle Street in the east, where renovation grants were made available to householders, with a clawback on resale for five years.

1980s

Work on the rehabilitation of Trinity 3 to MJP's plan for selective minor demolition, replacement new build, the creation of rear parking courtyards and refurbishment of the housing stock, was contracted out to Halsall Builders of Coombe End, Radstock. A plan for the diversion of traffic around the rear south west side of Vallis Way was drawn up by Somerset Highways, following on from an earlier suggestion by Rodney Goodall, and the Vallis Way diversion was endorsed and included in MJP's final design work.

MJP's plans were subsequently followed except for the closure and pedestrianisation of the diverted Vallis Way which was to be achieved by the creation of a widened road to the north east (the Baker Street Link). A significant amount of through traffic would inevitably have to continue to use Selwood Road, the shops at Badcox had to be serviced, and the Baker Street Link could not function as a bus route without a further acquisition and demolition of properties, which Mendip were not minded to implement.

In late 1983, I was appointed as the Area Planning Officer, responsible for east Mendip. It was evident at the outset that I had inherited a set of out of date and draft planning documents as the basis for managing development in the area; there was no up to date statutory plan to rely on to defend planning appeals or turn away clearly opportunistic development proposals.

In 1985, MJP were reappointed by Mendip to inform part of the work on a belated new Local Plan for Frome; to advise on the conservation implications of the continued protection of the Sun Street link road, or conversely whether that road had any real value in creating development opportunities in the Town and could be development led, given that there was no funding for it. The conclusions of this 1985 study by MJP led ultimately to the abandonment of the Sun Street link in the subsequent drafts of the Frome Local Plan, which was eventually adopted in 1991.

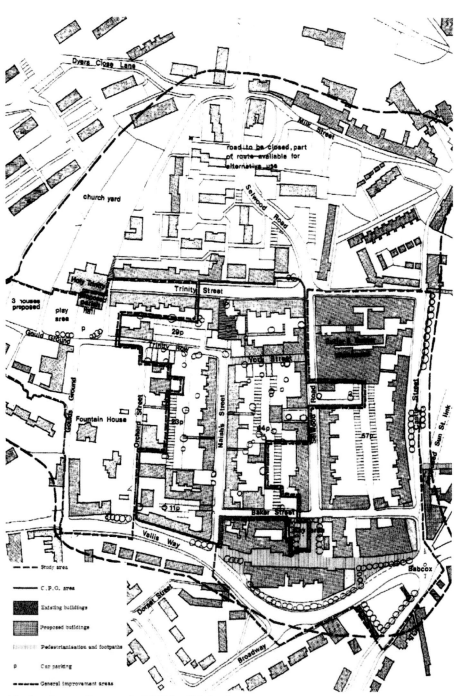

Moxley Jenner Proposals 1977 for Trinity 3

33

Work started on the Vallis Way diversion in 1986.

This change in planning policy with regard to the Sun Street link had prompted an opportunistic application in 1986 by the owner of most of the Piggeries land between Castle Street and Catherine Street for a private nursing home in the backland, which would have sterilised the peripheral sites owned by Mendip and those acquired for the Sun Street link road. We saw it simply as a valuation exercise: an attempt to inflate the property value and acquisition cost of the storage buildings and yards in the Piggeries. Peter Floyd of MJP and I represented Mendip at the subsequent planning appeal the following year. Fortunately, the case was dismissed, the appeal site was eventually acquired by agreement.

In March 1987, planning consent was granted to the Sun Street Conservation Group for the restoration of the properties at 2, 3, 4, 5, 6, 8 and 9 Sun Street on the abandoned road line.

In September 1987, I resigned as Area Planning Officer and joined livestock auctioneers and land agents Cooper and Tanner in Frome as an Associate Director at the time when the cattle market was being relocated to a purpose designed site at Standerwick. We were appointed to sell the Sun Street, Whittox Lane and two Castle Street properties which formed part of the abandoned road line. The Castle Street properties were bought and renovated by Pang Properties. Three of the Sun Street properties were renovated by the Sun Street Trust and sold on by Cooper and Tanner.

1990s

In 1991, Mendip submitted an outline planning application to redevelop the Piggeries site for housing and detailed approval was given in 1994 for the erection of 69 dwellings and the rebuilding of two existing houses. The remaining houses in Sun Street, 1,2,3, 4 and the Coach House were renovated by the MacLeay family and built out to an inspired scheme designed by local architect, Bruce Yoell in 1994, which won awards from William Stansell/Somerset Buildings Preservation Trust and the Federation of Master Builders. They are now listed Grade II.

The end of this decade saw the return of confidence and the final stages of the conservation of the Trinity area: Sun Street's housing had been restored, and the unfortunate phase 1 of the Trinity area redevelopment was planned to be partly demolished and redeveloped more sympathetically in a 1995 scheme by Knightstone Housing for 30 houses to replace the maisonettes and flats, but retaining the two storey houses at the eastern end of Trinity Street. The Piggeries housing scheme had been completed and subsequently received a design award from the Royal Town Planning Institute.

The imposing Byzantine styled former Butler and Tanner Print Works (1866) on Selwood Road had a chequered planning history in the previous decade. In 1980, proposals were made for its demolition, then light industrial use involving demolition of part of it and, next, an alternative use for the manufacture of carpets. Following a brief period of underuse as a warehouse/shoe retail outlet in the 1980s, speculative flat conversion schemes were proposed firstly for 91 elderly persons flats (refused), then for 66 flats (approved in 1991). A more satisfactory scheme was eventually granted consent in 1998 for conversion into 30 flats, again for Knightstone Housing Association, and built out by Halsall Builders of Radstock.

In the early 1990s Mendip's housing stock in the Trinity area was transferred to a housing association (then known as Mendip Housing) as part of a district wide asset sale in accordance with prevailing central government policy. Properties have subsequently been sold off and the loss of some of the renovated fabric is now evident – in the form of uPVC windows and doors – and the installation of satellite receiver dishes on prominent elevations have started to become noticeable as properties have changed hands. This is despite the Trinity area's designation as part of Frome's Conservation Area and also the statutory Grade II listing of some of the houses on Selwood Road and Castle Street, in particular, as being of architectural and historic interest.

A Jack the Ripper Scare

James Smith, a tramp was brought up in custody on remand charged with vagrancy. Grace Collins, a servant in the employ of Mrs Sheppard of Fromefield, said that on Friday last, shortly after 11am, the prisoner came to Mrs Sheppard's house and knocked on the front door. He had a dirty book in his hand and asked her to buy it, but she declined to do so. He then asked her for a trifle to help him on his way to Aldershot. She replied that she could not give him anything and he then said that, perhaps, the lady or gentleman of the house would help him. On telling him that they were engaged and could not see him, he put his foot inside the door and said he would insist upon seeing them. He also said: *No wonder Jack the Ripper is after you, you ****; I'm Jack the Ripper and I'll kill you.* He then removed his foot and she slammed the door. She ran into the breakfast room to see him off the premises, but afterwards went to the back gate for fear he would enter there. He swore at her and again said he would kill her if it was not for a year to come. He then took a knife from his pocket and drew it across his throat to show her how he would serve her. He remained there about ten minutes, cursing the whole time, and told her to be careful, as he would know her again. She told the Misses Sheppard and the gardener. Prisoner had his sleeves tucked up, carried his jacket on his arm, and had his hands and arms tattooed.

In the evening about 7.15, he returned again, when she was at the gate and she ran in and locked the door. He did not say anything to her then.

Fromefield House

Walter Sidney Joyce (13) and Emily Louisa Collins (13) gave corroborative evidence. They saw the prisoner near Mrs Sheppard's house on Friday morning and heard him swear. Joyce heard him mention Jack the Ripper and Collins heard him say he would twist Mrs Sheppard's servant's neck. Sergeant Mason said that on Saturday at 9am, he went to the Workhouse and found the prisoner breaking stones. He took him and another man to Fromefield and Grace Collins at once recognised him as the one who had threatened her on the previous day. He then charged him with vagrancy and using threats. He had tattoo marks on his hands and arms. Prisoner protested that he was not the man and that the charge had been trumped up. The magistrates said that it was a very bad case, to go frightening people in private houses in that way. He would be sent to Shepton Mallet gaol for 21 days with hard labour.

My thanks to Clive Wilkins for this report from the Somerset and Wiltshire Journal, 21 September 1889. Ed

From the Czar's Palace, St Petersburg
to a Charity Shop in Whittox Lane, Frome
A brief life of the Hon Alexandrine Perceval Ouseley (1814-1863)
Follower of the Revd WJE Bennett
by ALM

Alexandrine Perceval Ouseley's father, Sir Gore Ouseley, was Ambassador-Extraordinary to the Persian court where he was involved in mediating a dispute between Persia and Russia, which concluded with a treaty in 1813. He was awarded a decoration by the Persians and left for Russia in 1814.[1] It

was at St Petersburg where Sir Gore was awarded the Grand Cordon of the Order of St Alexander Nevsky by Czar Alexander I. It is not known how long the family remained in Russia but Alexandrine[2] was born there during the visit and named after the Czar who was her Godfather and Sponsor at her baptism.

In London the Ouseley family home was in the parish of St Paul's Knightsbridge where Rev WJE Bennett's controversial ministry ended in 1851. Alexandrine and her sister involved themselves in parish charitable work and provided funds for the building of St Barnabas church, Pimlico, founded by Bennett. The Rev Bennett, exhausted as a result of his protracted

The Grand Cordon of the Order of St Alexander Nevsky

disagreements with the Bishop of London and the riotous behaviour of the mobs[3] in Pimlico left England to recuperate at Kissingen, Bavaria. Travelling with him were his son and a church warden from St Barnabas, Sir John Harrington. Before and after Kissingen, where he took the waters and remained for five weeks, he visited other towns in Germany and in Belgium, Austria and Italy.

The Frome living, which had become vacant, was in the gift of the Marquess of Bath who was then under age. His mother who acted on her son's behalf offered it to Bennett, who accepted in December 1851. The vicar arrived in Frome and, according to one report, his induction was carried out in unseemly haste to avoid parishioners challenging the appointment. However, a petition objecting to the appointment, signed by a few dozen persons was sent to the Bishop of Bath and Wells and to Lady Bath who replied that the appointment had been made and could not be revoked. There were reports that Lady Bath had stones and eggs thrown at her when the induction ceremony took place on 24 January 1852.

Alexandrine Ouseley and her sister Mary, eight years her senior removed to Frome soon after Rev Bennett. They settled in Conigar House which became the centre of their charitable work. According to J W Singer[4] the house was extended to cater for their charitable activities that included a home and school in Whittox Lane for poor girls. At the census in 1861, the 'Home School' at 26 Chappell Street, (Whittox Lane) Frome listed 13 female pupils from 8 to 15 years of age[5] with Miss Mary Anderson, born in London, aged 27 as 'servant in charge.'

Conigar House

The current 26 Whittox Lane has the light-coloured door in the centre

Miss A Ouseley's compassion didn't extend to an eleven year old boy whom she confronted in her pew at St John's Church in December 1852. She told him to sit elsewhere but noticed his hand on her prayer book which she later discovered had disappeared. Henry Vincent, a pawnbroker said the boy, Francis Roper, brought two books into his shop on 13 December for which he advanced 4d. Vincent contacted the parish clerk when he discovered that one of the books bore the name of Miss Ouseley, who decided to prosecute. At the committal hearing on 15 December the Bench was informed that Francis Roper had twice previously been to gaol. On the last occasion, for stealing from a shop, he was sentenced to three months in prison and a flogging. In January 1853 Francis appeared before the magistrates and said he took the book 'for want of bread' and he hoped his Worship would send him to a Penitentiary. The Chairman, in addressing the prisoner said that he noted that his father was a felon and that his mother[6] was 'an abandoned creature.' He understood that the boy had been sent out to steal by his parents.

Francis Roper was sentenced to two years imprisonment, but the Chairman said he would, use his 'influence to get him in the Philanthropic Institution where his morals could be cared for and he could be taught a trade, whereby he would be enabled in after years to earn an honest livelihood.'[7]

Miss A Ouseley opened a charity shop in Whittox Lane that sold clothing at reduced prices for the poor, some of it made by the girls at the school. Here she would serve behind the counter; it was her policy that the poor should make a payment for the items sold in the shop rather than be given the clothing free of charge. The sisters also visited the sick in their homes and on Sundays took charge of up to 100 children whose parents attended divine service at the parish church. They also gave generous financial help towards the restoration of the parish church being carried out by Rev Bennett.

Mary Jane Ouseley died in July 1861 aged 54. Alexandrine died on 1 December 1863 aged 48.[8] The additional work after her sister's death was, according to Singer, a great strain on Miss Ouseley's health. She was buried in St John's churchyard. The Rev Bennett didn't usually perform funeral services, but did so on this occasion in a tribute to the deceased.

The local press[9] in reporting the restoration work at St Johns noted '...the spire was completed last week and the whole of the aisle windows completed'. The window near the north side west door is a memorial to Mary Jane Ouseley, the second one to Alexandrine Perceval Ouseley. The windows were executed by Hardman of Birmingham.

The windows in St John's Church in memory of Alexandrine Perceval Ouseley and her sister Mary Jane Ouseley are the second and third from the north west door respectively. They were originally by Hardman of Birmingham depicting Mary visiting Elizabeth and the Naming of John the Baptist and are shown in the line drawings. They were replaced in the 1920s with stained glass by Kempe as shown.

My thanks to Rev Colin Alsbury for this information and for permission to reproduce these illustrations. Ed

[1] *The Dictionary of National Biography fails to explain why he went to Russia though it was most likely   to receive the gratitude of Czar Alexander and the decoration*
[2] *She was given her second name, Perceval after one of her godmothers, Mrs Spencer Perceval, widow of the assassinated Prime Minister Spencer Perceval (Austin)*
[3] *Sir Frederick Ouseley, a curate at St Barnabas and brother of the sisters was assaulted and threatened in the street. In a letter to Rev John Rich, 20 Nov 1850, he wrote "... we had reason to be certain of a more violent attack on the 17th so we took every precaution ...at 10am the mob began to collect, but luckily our own congregation were seated in time. Nothing in the church happened before the sermon but during it a prodigious yell was heard without, which frightened some of our people much. The church was crammed to suffocation and a body of staunch friends were stationed in the nave to prevent any attack .... When the sermon was concluded, and the non-communicants prepared to retire, a violent rush was made by the populace outside; ... had they succeeded in their*

attempt our beautiful edifice would have been dismantled... 100 policemen succeeded in quelling the mob without, sufficiently to let the congregation retire. The organist by my direction played "full organ" to drown the row. In about 40 minutes the church was cleared. "(Text of letter quoted from the life of Rev Sir F A G Ouseley)

[4] Singer wrote a biographical note on the Ouseley sisters, published in the Somerset Standard in 1893. He noted that Miss A Ouseley was the driving force in the partnership
[5] Five girls were from Frome, three from 'Somerset' one each from Devizes, Andover, Warminster and Glamorgan, one no birth place given
[6] According to the 1851 census Mrs Elizabeth Roper, of Paul Street, his mother was aged 31. She was a widow with three children. Occupation described as 'pauper nurse'
[7] Francis Roper's time in a Philanthropic Institution, if indeed he attended one was apparently put to good use as he prospered. In 1861 aged 21 and single he was in lodgings at Upton Lovell and employed as a Power Loom Weaver in a Woollen Mill. By 1871 he was married to Mary Papps living at Highworth with two children, occupation: Engine Fitter. In 1881 he was at Highbridge with wife and four children, occupation: Engineer Mechanic. In 1891 at Burnham he was self-employed as Engineer Machinist. In 1901 he was at Street as a self-employed Mechanical Engineer and in 1911 a self-employed Engineer Iron & Brass Founder. He died in 1918 aged 78 leaving estate worth £3,348, his wife died in 1921 aged 79
[8] She left estate worth £14,000. Rev Bennett was the sole executor
[9] Frome Times 2 November 1864

The 'late alarming Riots', Frome 1796

ONE HUNDRED POUNDS REWARD

Whereas divers letters have lately been sent to Mr THOMAS BALNE, the Constable of the Hundred and Town of FROME, threatening to set fire to his House and to assassinate him, which letters, it is apprehended, have been sent to him in consequence of his having exerted himself in the due execution of his office, in suppressing some late alarming Riots in the said town. We, whose names are hereunto subscribed, being impressed with the necessity of supporting the Peace Officers of the Town, and encouraging them in the proper discharge of their duty, do hereby offer a reward of ONE HUNDRED POUNDS to any person who will discover the person or persons who wrote all or either of the said letters, so that he, she, or they may be convicted of the said offence. *Signed W Ireland, vicar and 79 names*

Frome, 22 April, 1796

We, whose Names are hereunto subscribed, Inhabitants of the Town and neighbourhood of FROME, do hereby vote our unanimous thanks to Lieut HARRIS, commanding a detachment of the ESSEX LIGHT DRAGOONS, and to the Quarter-Master and Privates of the said detachment, for the zeal and alacrity shewn by them in quelling the late alarming RIOT, in the said Town. And we also vote the like thanks to Lieut MORRISH, of the Marines, and Lieut ROBINSON, of the 40th regiment of foot, for their zeal and services on that occasion.

Signed by the same 80 names plus T BALNE, Constable and K J BARBER

Frome, 22 April, 1796

'We are sorry to learn, from a correspondent at Frome, that the tranquillity of that town was, a few days since, violently disturbed by a multitude of Mendip colliers and other people from the country, who entered the town armed with bludgeons, and endeavoured to lay the bakers under a requisition to sell bread at a reduced price. On non-compliance they mistreated one baker in a violent degree, and, had it not been for the vigilance of the Chief Constable in calling in the aid of a party of the Essex Light Dragoons quartered there, and for their *good conduct* on that occasion, it is much to be apprehended that murder would have ensued. Many of the colliers violently assaulted the soldiery, who, in their own defence, were driven to the necessity of having recourse to their sabres and tho' blood was spilt, we are happy to relate that there were no lives lost. In the evening the mob repaired to the house of another baker in the town, broke all his windows, and did other damage, but quietness, we hear, has now again resumed her seat in the town. The Constable has, since the above happened, received some anonymous letters in consequence of his having exerted himself in the execution of his office in quelling the mob, threatening to set fire to his house and to murder him. *See the advertisement above*

WHEREAS several scandalous and malicious Reports have lately been circulated in ROAD and the towns of FROME and TROWBRIDGE, and the neighbouring places, tending to impress the minds of the people with a belief that I, JOSEPH CABELL of Road in the County of Somerset, Baker, have been an active instrument in endeavouring to induce the Farmers to ENHANCE THE PRICE OF WHEAT, and likewise, in endeavouring to encourage the Bakers in the towns of Bradford and Trowbridge, to keep down the weight of Bread, and other reports equally injurious to my character:

A reward of TEN GUINEAS is hereby offered to any person or persons who will discover the author or authors of the above reports, so that he, she, or they may be brought to Justice; the above reward will be paid on conviction by me.

JOSEPH CABELL

Road, 20 April, 1796

My thanks to Clive Wilkins for these four related extracts from the Bath Chronicle, April, 1796. Ed

Evelyn Waugh in Nunney
by Adrie van der Luijt

Evelyn Waugh

In 1936 Evelyn Waugh had finally been granted an annulment of his marriage to his first wife Evelyn Gardner ('She-Evelyn'). After an initial meeting in Portofino, he had fallen in love with Laura Herbert. He proposed marriage, by letter, in Spring 1936. There were initial misgivings from the Herberts, an aristocratic Catholic family; as a further complication, Laura Herbert was a cousin of Evelyn Gardner. Despite some family hostility, the marriage took place on 17 April 1937. As a wedding present the bride's grandmother bought the couple Piers Court, a country house near Stinchcombe in Gloucestershire. However, in the preceding months Waugh had been house hunting in Somerset, arriving by train in Frome on 14 September 1936 and staying in Mells. On the recommendation of a friend, he looked at properties in Nunney and Whatley a week later, in the afternoon of Monday 21 September 1936.

He wrote in his diary: 'Whatley Rectory is quite agreeable, but like a thousand other houses in England. No decent drawing room. The housekeeper Mrs Haynes showed us over. I asked of a tap whether it was hot or cold water. *I must ask the canon. Why not try? Oh no water ever comes out.'*

He found Manor Farm House in Nunney much more to his taste. 'The house at Nunney is enchanting,' he wrote. 'Very small, next to the castle and farm buildings. Exquisite 18th century façade. Castle excellent and whole village very attractive.' 'I went to the door and asked if it was for sale. A pretty girl came and said*: How* did *you know? We only decided at luncheon today. We haven't yet given our notice.* She, her mother and apparently some other relatives sublease it from Mr Young the farmer on condition he keeps a room there.'

'Inside and out it is very dilapidated but of the highest beauty. Panelled rooms, very fine oak and walnut staircase, Norman cellars. For a considerable sum it could be made one of the loveliest small houses in England. 'Walking back, I met Trim who had motored out to meet me. We went back to the house and met the farmer. A shock, as he's young and a gentleman. I imagined putting him up in a bungalow, but clearly that won't wash.' Later that week Evelyn Waugh looked at Manor Farm House again, this time accompanied by Laura Herbert's mother, Mary. They also took a second look at the rectory at Whatley. The next day he drove to London, only to jump on a train back to

Frome at 9am on Saturday morning to show both properties to Laura. 'Delightful day, though wet. Went to look at Whatley rectory and Nunney Farm. Laura seemed to like farm. Lunched and dined at (Mells) Manor'.

After Laura went back to London on the Monday, Evelyn Waugh wrote to Major Linton Shore, the owner of Manor Farm House in Nunney who lived 2 miles down the road at Whatley House. A reply arrived the next day, but Waugh described it was 'unsatisfactory'. On Wednesday 30 September 1936 he went to see another house in Nunney, belonging to the Wilbraham family. This was Nunney Court on Donkey Lane, which a few years later would be substantially enlarged by new owners, the Andersons. Waugh described it as 'poky but pretty'. Another unidentified property proved 'wholly unsuitable'.

An aerial shot of Nunney taken in 1931, shows Manor Farm House to the left of Nunney Castle

Upon his return to London, Evelyn Waugh received the 'grand news' on 5 October that Major Linton Shore was, in principle, prepared to let him have Manor Farm House. However, Shore was not prepared to sell and would only agree to let the property on a long-term lease if Waugh took on 40 acres of land as well. Evelyn Waugh returned to Nunney a week later to see Young the farmer. 'He was very good-natured and eager to convenience everybody,' Waugh wrote in his diary. 'Saw Linton Shore who is a footler but not the bully I had expected.'

After another week in London he travelled to Frome on a 'very bad train' and took Lady Horner of Mells Manor over to Nunney the day before she relocated to London for the winter. Yet another visit to Nunney followed the next day, on Friday 23 October. Evidently still keen to purchase the Manor Farm House in Nunney, Waugh wrote to Major Linton Shore and offered him a down payment of £3,000 for the lease plus £50 a year for seven years and then £150. He also proposed to buy the Wilbraham's house in exchange. 'During seven years I will spend not less than £700 a year in restoration,' Evelyn Waugh wrote to Major Linton Shore. Based on the Retail Price Index this is around £37,000 in today's money, or £108,000 when the comparison is based on average wages.

Weeks went by without a response from Shore. Increasingly frustrated, Evelyn Waugh returned to the West Country and started looking at other properties, such as Warminster Manor ('beastly surroundings'). He returned to London with his heart still firmly set on Nunney.

On Sunday 15 November 1936 Evelyn Waugh wrote again to Major Shore, this time offering to buy the Nunney property but withdrawing his offer to take on the long-term lease. Still without a reply, he continued to travel up and down between London and Somerset, looking at various 'no-good' properties in Batcombe, Stroud and other places but feeling 'cold, tired and very low spirited'.

On Monday 21 December Evelyn Waugh took his first look at Piers Court in Stinchcombe, Gloucestershire, describing it as 'absolutely first-rate'. The Grade II-listed building is surrounded by 23 acres of land.

Piers Court in Stinchcombe

After Laura's grandmother offered to buy the house as a wedding present, Evelyn Waugh's offer of £3,350 for the Stinchcombe ('Stinkers') property was accepted in January 1937. He lived in Piers Court from 1937 to 1956, during which time he produced works including Brideshead Revisited. Waugh died at Combe Florey in Somerset in 1966.

Major Linton Shore never got back to him about the Nunney property.

This is a shortened version of an article by Adrie van der Luijt on the Visit Nunney *website. Ed*

Minding the Monarch's Way
by Richard Wallis

Chris Billinghurst's talk to the Frome Society on 15 December 2018 on the Monarch's Way, which follows a 625-mile journey by the future Charles II from the site of the battle of Worcester to Shoreham, brought back memories of my own experiences as a 'minder' of the Way. Trevor Antill, who designed this long-distance walk, advertised for volunteers to help him keep an eye on it and I joined Trevor's Happy Band of Minders in 1997 when I took on the Wells to Castle Cary section. He warned me that some of the paths were little used. How right he was.

For several miles the walking was easy enough but then came the first problem: a fifty-yard stretch of nettles. I used to put on overtrousers, rainproof jacket and hedging gloves to get through. The nettles were five feet tall and would sting through anything less. That was soon followed by a green lane which turned to swamp at the slightest fall of rain. After that came a thorn hedge. I had to crawl through on my stomach. I'm not making this up, honestly! Walking along the Fosseway for half a mile was straightforward, once you'd got used to the huge lorries roaring past your elbow.

Am I making it sound dreadful? I loved it. It was a challenge I relished. E-mails began to fly between Trevor, County and myself and slowly, slowly, things improved.

Traffic on the Fosseway was getting heavier every year and Trevor pressed for paths in West Bradley to be opened up. It had been a no-go area for some time, a situation not helped by the fact that it was a parish with no Council. Responsibility passed to Mendip District Council. Their Footpath Officer and her team set about the entire parish. A new route was opened in 2002, avoiding the Fosseway.

Richard dressed for walking

One of the pleasures of the walk was meeting people. A farmer gave me a lesson in hedge laying. The new route took you past aircraft hangars; the owner offered me a spin in his plane. A man with a dog at an isolated house was amazed that the path outside his gate offered a 625 mile 'walkies.' One year, from Pennard Hill, I had a great view down on to the Glastonbury Festival site; another, I travelled with a hundred or so of the visitors. But the best of my encounters was meeting up with Trevor at the Apple Tree inn, swapping Travellers' Tales for an hour over lunch.

Occasionally it was clear that human relationships along the Way were not all sweetness and light. A letter appeared on a post outside a pig farm, put up by the owner. It was from a vet and said, 'I called without warning as a result of complaints about ill-treatment of animals. I found nothing wrong.' Evidently some bad feeling in the air, as well as the pungent odour.

Another year, another notice, this one by a churned-up plot of land between two houses. 'Planning application for the development of this site was refused...and is currently under appeal...the wanton destruction of this site is an unethical attempt by the owner to influence the decision.'

Even I did not totally escape aggravation. I had just crossed the Fosseway and was beating down some vegetation, trying to find a footbridge, when a car pulled up, a large young woman got out and dashed over the road, shouting crossly, 'What are you doing?' She was a farmer's wife. She pointed to a large barn just behind us and told me it had been broken into twice and expensive farm machinery stolen. I assume from her outburst she thought this old man with rucksack and stick she'd spotted, was sussing out the place for a third burglary! Anyway, she seemed to find my explanation that I was following in the footsteps of Charles II so far out that it was believable and we parted amicably.

The years went by and one by one problems were resolved...except for Hornblotton. Its path number is engraved on my heart, SM 20/11. In 1997 Trevor's instructions read 'should this path have been opened up, please use it.' It hadn't. The following year the County Footpath Officer told us, 'I hope to resolve this as soon as possible.'

I discovered a little broken-down wicket gate which I could scramble through, on hands and knees. A belt of thorn and bramble soon made this unusable. In 2005 this was cleared. In 2006 a stile was erected, so one end was now open. In 2007 Trevor found 'substantial works being carried out, and new fencing'. A fine fence it was, but in putting it up, the stile had been demolished. So the path was blocked again. Trevor complained. The reply from County promised action. There followed another missive, 'I cannot get any reply from the landowner.' My annual visit in June 2009 found a flimsy stile at one end, a padlocked gate at the other.

March 2010. The owners are written to and asked to remove the padlock *as soon as possible*. Where had we heard that before? A little later a small parcel arrives from Trevor. Inside is a monogrammed Golden Duster. A lady member had prepared one for every Minder. I sleep with it under my pillow.

June 2010. Flimsy stile replaced with sturdier version, but...there's a barbed wire fence just beyond!...and the padlock is still there.

Sadly, Trevor's untimely death meant that he never saw the end of this saga of obstruction, though end it did, in 2011. It had taken 15 years! What an extraordinary memorial he has left, something not just to remember him by, but a gift from him to all those who will be following in his footsteps.

I wish 'good walking' to everyone who will be treading the path I got to know so well.

A Morning at the Parish Soup Kitchen, Froome-Selwood

It is no ordinary curiosity that finds me at the Soup Kitchen this morning for the first time. On entering, I am greeted kindly by four ladies, who tell me they are preparing for work. They think, by the number of names sent in by the Vicar, that there will be a great many of the poor here today. One shows me a boiler which is nearly full of most excellent pea soup. I taste it, and am certain that no epicure, however dainty, would refuse it at his table. Another fastens on a brown Holland apron. (Prudent being: she knows that what she is about to do will soil her dress unless she takes this necessary precaution). But hark! The clock of the Old Church strikes eleven; and now a small window communicating with the lobby outside the kitchen is opened. A tin can appears upon the ledge, given by a poor woman to the lady with the apron, who having learned from the one who is engaged at the window in collecting soup kitchen tickets and pence that this poor woman has bought a ticket and a penny takes it to the boiler and has a quart of soup put into it, which, with half a pound of bread, taken from a table that is covered with small loaves, she gives to the poor woman, who leaves the kitchen for her house, where no doubt she enjoys a heavy meal.

This goes on until half past twelve when there is a lull. The soup is nearly all gone, and so is the bread, and now, for a few minutes, all rest, and turn their attention to a small dog, whose thin skin and slight form remind her that the stone hearth of the soup kitchen is not so warm as the rug in her master's house, so she has curled herself up in the skirts of a French merino. But see; she hears footsteps, and greatly to the amusement of all, sets up a shrill barking, which is not continued long- her throat is sore. And now the poor begin to pour in again. These come from far, some have large families and bring two tickets, for which they receive two quarts of soup and one pound of bread.

At last the clock strikes one: the footsteps of the last poor woman have died away, the table is nearly cleared of its weight of bread; there are only a few who have not come, no doubt they have good reasons; the window is shut, and the morning's business nearly over; the ladies at the window count the pence and tickets, compare notes, and find that all is correct- their lists tally. I am bold enough to ask how often this is repeated, and am told- every Wednesday and Saturday during the winter months from eleven till one; that any person can have thirty soup tickets for 5s. Subscribed; and that for every ticket and penny brought by the poor, provided they attend the Old Church and conform to the rules regulating the soup kitchen, one quart of soup and half a pound of bread may be received.

My morning at the soup kitchen is over, and I bid adieu- au revoir- to the kind Christians who have spent their morning in administering to the wants of the poor; and on my way home I wonder if in other parishes, as in ours, there are to be found as many warm hearts, who, from morn till eve, are willing to spend their time and do spend it, in doing works of charity. God grant that I may be wrong when I say that I do not think that such is the case in *every* parish.

My thanks to ALM for this article from the Frome Times, 18 February 1863. Ed

'Farthing Bundles' Part III from the Autobiography of Clara Grant

Clara Grant

Our Frome home for nearly forty years was in North Parade, and I remember well our first evening in it. My little brother and I took a candle and explored the whole house, which, with its three flights of stairs and about a dozen rooms, seemed to us a magic palace, but it was awkward to work. The stairs were steep and the landings tiny, but they helped in our training, since it was a rule that everybody big enough, male or female, carried up, as far as they went, any load found resting at any stage. That was typical of the kind of training my mother gave us and for which she was famous. The following lines of 'A Good Housekeeper' might well have been written for her:

How shall I tell her? By her cellar: Cleanly shelves and whitened wall. And with pleasure Take her measure. By the way she keeps her brooms, Or the peeping At the keeping Of her back and unseen rooms, By her kitchen's air of neatness, And its general completeness, Where in cleanliness and sweetness The rose of order blooms.

She hated the showy and shoddy, and made us feel that a smart drawing room with a dirty scullery is a vulgar thing. As there were nine of us method and order were essential, and my mother was a wonderful organiser in her own sphere. It takes time to establish a method, but it usually saves time in the long run. Our Old Clothes Department in Fern Street owes much to her teaching, and nowhere does order count more than in a large elementary school. A carefully planned routine in small things wisely enforced becomes habitual, and, in time, automatic; it is soothing and restful, and saves time and energy for more important things.

Being a bookworm, I hated all housework, and one day, when by no means 'dashing away with the smoothing iron', I snapped out 'I don't like housework,' to which my mother replied 'I shall have to **make** you like it.' Well endowed with the Grant instinct for arguing, I replied 'I think you can make me **do** it, mother, but I don't think you can make me **like** it,' and my father, sitting there reading, said, riskily, 'Well, and I suppose the child is right.' Nothing happened.

My mother's 'Yea' was 'Yea' and her 'Nay' was 'Nay', but I remember no repressions which created resentment or complexes. Essential habits were established from the first. Once in bed no artificial howls ever effected a transfer to the warm dining-room below, such as maddened my mother in other homes. But, of course, not even my mother could 'make us sleep.' Frolics were safe until two rows of us in nighties filled the windows in search of further excitement, and as that would shock our respectable Parade my mother would quickly ascend and become active.

Occasionally, probably on colder nights, we sought from each other solutions of the great mysteries of the universe. 'I say, supposing all the people in the world were dead 'cept one, who'd bury that one?' No sound. No light. Finally, as so often happens, the questioner had to find his own solution. 'I expect God would send an angel down from heaven to bury that one.' My mother, on occasion, would be more helpful. 'Do you think,' asked one, 'we shall have all we want when we get to heaven?' 'Well, I can't say that we shall have all we want there, but I do believe that what we can't have we shan't want.' Small one, unsatisfied, 'Well, I hope I shall have a jackplane.'

For table manners we received a penny for memorising the following precepts, and something different for disobeying them:

TABLE RULES FOR LITTLE FOLKS

In silence I must take my seat, And give God thanks before I eat; Must for my food in patience wait, Till I am asked to hand my plate; I must not scold, nor whine, nor pout, Nor move my chair nor plate about; I must not speak a useless word. For children must be seen –not heard; I must not talk about my food. Nor fret if I don't think it good; I must not say , 'The bread is old,' 'The tea is hot,' 'the coffee cold;' My mouth with food I must not crowd, Nor while I'm eating speak aloud; The table cloth I must not spoil, Nor with my food my fingers soil; Must keep my seat when I have done, Nor round the table sport or run; When told to rise, then I must put My chair away with noiseless foot; And lift my heart to God above, In praise for all His wondrous love.

We were rarely bored. We created interesting little games and occupations for ourselves and did not resent geography in the guise of Happy Family, and we had, of course, the irreplaceable education and stimulus of our own large 'Happy Family.'

Sundays were never Sabbatarian, though I remember once picking up my crochet inadvertently and dropping it like a hot coal when I realised my breach of a commandment. Crochet would seem to be a delightfully pensive Sunday occupation if only one does not crochet all the week, but we were curiously inconsistent in those days. My father was shocked one Sunday to hear us singing the duet, 'My true love hath my heart,' but he would enjoy a joke if it were only spoken instead of sung, and his dear old mother was horrified one Sunday to hear me playing, 'God save the Queen,' and my 'But, Granny, it is a prayer' was of no avail. On this point it is interesting to read that when the Bishop of London visited the trenches, on not a few occasions the whole body of men sang 'Amen' instinctively at the end of 'God save the King.'

Once, too, at a musical examination at an elementary school in Marlborough, in 1873, an HMI refused to hear the National Anthem and 'God bless the Prince of Wales,' as he could not examine anything with the name of God in it in secular hours.

On Sunday evenings we children played 'Church' with the paternal armchair as pulpit, and one evening when I was preaching the pulpit collapsed, and evensong ended in most unseemly hilarity. External treats were few and enjoyed all the more. There were drives for business or pleasure, on which we were taken in turn, our special joy lying in coming home late. On Fair Days my father would take us to the Fair, and then at intervals would come Sanger's Circus with its great procession through the town, a 'truly elegant cavalcade' of gay riders and gilded chariots with crowned ladies, War Arabs, Peruvian God Horses, and other wondrous sights. At night my father would take us to the circus, but I hated seeing animals (as I later hated seeing children) doing unnatural things, so I had the money instead.

My father found in us a delightful excuse for sharing these excitements. He thoroughly enjoyed them, and, like Burne-Jones, he revelled in Punch and Judy, just as we found him, at 73, wrapt in the 'Arabian Nights.' But his great passion was music, and, though he had but three months' lessons in his life, he was organist for over fifty years, playing both at Chapmanslade and Berkley Churches, walking into Frome after his Berkley evensong to hear the concluding voluntary at St John's. Finding it impossible to continue his country work after removing to Frome, he became organist at Wesley Chapel, where the authorities gave him generous scope for his enthusiasm. The organ was three times enlarged, finally by my brother, to five complete organs, four manuals and 2220 pipes, which it took four men to blow for Dr Frederick Bridge, organist of Westminster Abbey, who came down to open it.

Dr Bridge stayed with us and proved a delightful guest. I remember how he enjoyed the wild flowers with which we had graced the table. When he was writing in my album, I said 'what a pity you can't write your initials in music as I can.' He wrote at once a Fuga 'JF Bridge' using bars and rests where notes failed, and the following verse:

This little Fugue subject I write down in Frome, Ere I pack up my traps for Home, sweet Home. The chorus and organ I leave all at rest. By the Blowers at least my departure is blest.

My father's oratorio services and classical concerts were famous for thirty years, and probably rarely has so much Catholic Mass Music re-echoed from a Wesleyan temple. Once annually did my father fail at his post. No Watchnight Service on New Year's Eve was complete without a certain hymn of Charles Wesley's, one of the original collection of which John Wesley wrote, 'Here are both the purity, the strength and the elegance of the English language, and, at the same time, the utmost simplicity and plainness, suited to every capacity.' The hymn ran—literally ran—as follows: '*Come let us anew Our journey pursue. Roll round with the year. And never stand still Till the Master appear.*' Even its tune was 'Derby,' and it, too, its journey pursued, up hill and down dale and never stood still, and my father absented himself, refusing to play anything so unmusical, until one historic Sunday morning it was given out in chapel and, for once, my father was unhappy on an organ stool.

Personally, I regret that he did not lend his wonderful gift of expressive accompaniment to the making of those pious resolutions, and, perchance, to the swelling of that triumphant throng pictured in the final verse: *'O that each from his Lord May receive the glad word. Well and faithfully done; Enter into My joy, and sit down on My throne.'*

In 1904, when Sir Frederick Bridge was editing the music of the new Methodist Hymn Book, he also looked askance at 'Derby.' Wishing to satisfy popular sentiment, he asked his old housekeeper, a devout Wesleyan, to sing it to him, and once more the old hymn its journey pursued, this time through the kitchen speaking tube, whereupon the Doctor with his masterly hand put the curb on and it now pursues a more even tenor of its way. An organist of the temperament and almost unbridled enthusiasm of my father must have often been a sore trial to the authorities, but our Wesleyan friends gave him his chance and I am grateful, as I am to those great Wesleys who woke up my own church in the 18th century.

Our house reflected music from many walls. 'What is that picture?' asked a well-known legal worthy of my father. On hearing that it was Beethoven playing to a group of enraptured friends, he said, 'Hm, I thought it was a meeting of creditors!'

To my father Handel was the greatest 'great master,' and he rarely missed a Handel Festival. My brother is named George Frederick after him, and I after Clara Novello, a great Handelian singer of whom Mrs Craik (author of 'John Halifax, Gentleman') always felt, when listening to her singing of 'I know that my redeemer liveth,' that she was performing an 'act of faith.'

I had a beautiful voice as a child, but hard practice in my father's choral classes, followed by nearly five years of teaching in a schoolroom crowded with classes, crushed all my hopes of emulating my namesake, and those laurels fell to my sister Bessie, so well known and popular as a singer, and to my sister, Harriet, now in my own profession, and helping Dr Hayward in his interesting 'Celebrations.'

A VICTORIAN PRIVATE SCHOOL

At seven we went to the National School for one year, of which my only memory is of my passionate protest, before the whole school, against the injustice of keeping us all in for an unconfessed sin committed by one. I was borne away to a dark cubbyhole by the head mistress, beating a tattoo on her person en route. I worked off a lot of steam in my childhood, perhaps happily for my many foes in later life.

For the next five years we attended a Seminary for Young Ladies in Fromefield, the proprietor of which used to advertise quarterly when 'School Duties would be resumed, DV.' There were 6-8 boarders and 15-20 day pupils, and one assistant governess who took small groups of pupils in the dining-room. The main schoolroom (and cloakroom) was a very small back room, whilst the largest room in the house was a stately drawing-room apparently rarely used except for interviewing parents, but which, of course, should have been the schoolroom.

The National School, Bath Street, built 1825, demolished 1974

We learned everything by rote, mainly out of dry-as-dust manuals. So long as the allotted portion was accurately repeated nothing further was asked. Bible exercises consisted of a chapter read verse by verse round the table in which it was usually, but not always, safe to calculate one's turn and be mentally free 'in between.' We read history from Mrs Markham, again without comment, and in the 'Child's Guide to Knowledge, Adapted for Young Persons by a Lady' (640 pages) we rushed breathlessly over the universe with 'no woodcuts or engravings to take off the attention,' since 'the simplicity of the language rendered picture illustration altogether unnecessary.' The form was that of question and answer, and occasionally the author would mercifully place all the information in the question thus, 'Does not this offer considerable resistance to the formidable artillery invented by Sir William Armstrong?' and we would answer glibly 'Yes.' Mispronunciation of 'indigenous' or 'subterraneous' would be corrected, misunderstandings never.

'A Lady' was no Prohibitionist, for she devoted sixteen pages to wines and spirits, and one hopes the book was not circulated abroad since we learned that 'God has made England the most powerful of all nations.'

There was absolutely no scope for intelligence, and I, having a good memory and often feeling bored, was once caught reading a story book. Miss C was capable of shrewd sarcasm at times. 'If your mother does not mind you reading story books here I do not mind.' 'Have your nails lost their parents?' she would say; 'I notice they are in deep mourning.'

Spelling, without meanings, was the opening afternoon exercise and was worked on the exhaustive method, the last in the race fitting in the final letters and 'going up.' Spelling victories were my one joy, and once, arriving late I bounced into the room only to be told to 'go out again and come in properly.' Shirking this humiliation, I spent a long afternoon in the hall, with its main objects of interest: the rocking horse on which we never rocked and the ancient tall hat and stick of Grandfather C (long in his grave) hanging there, we said, to rouse in burglars the fear of the man in the house. At closing time I calmly walked into the study, took my hat and went home.

I used to think Miss C was afraid of me, but I fancy she had subtle methods of achieving her victories whilst conserving her energy. Needless to say, in none of the above trials did I seek the maternal sanction or sympathy.

Certain facts are more easily memorised in early years, and we learned 'for life' our tables, many spellings, the monarchs of England, their dates and their spouses, and any facts learned by rote which struck our fancy, but of real, vital education there was none.

We had no physical training, no nature study, no literature in its real sense, and we were told nothing of that history of our town of which Frome is so justly proud. We were never told that Christina Rossetti lived next door, nor taught any of her poems beloved by children. All we knew of 'next door' was that the fattest man in Frome lived there and that he once had the whooping cough.

Similarly, as we did not attend St John's Church, we were told nothing by anyone of the wonderful spiritual adventure which made it historic, but occasionally we would peep into that treasure house of beauty on Procession Nights and see the 'Old Vicar' marching round in his wonderful cope with radiating symbolic design, known to us only as 'the old gold mantle with the clock on the back.'

In true education we lead from the 'here' to the 'near' to the 'far.' I have heard it whispered, 'tell it in Gath' that the Oxford Movement has been expounded in Frome with no reference whatever to that Tractarian citadel and giant: St John's and Mr Bennett.

Extracts from 'Farthing Bundles', the Autobiography of Clara Grant, Parts I and II, were published in FSLS Yearbooks 19, 2016 and 20, 2017 respectively. Ed

Early Camera Clubs in Frome Part II
by ALM

Frome Camera Club 1898-1899

An advertisement appeared in the Somerset Standard (SS) of 25 March 1898 inviting all interested persons to attend a meeting that evening at the Temperance Hall to consider the desirability of forming a camera club, with Dr Dalby in the chair.

Dr Augustus W Dalby (1860-1915), Gentle Street, Frome

Opening the meeting the Chairman said sundry camera men thought it desirable to form a club. There had been one in Frome some years ago which was very useful to those who belonged to it. A club provided the opportunity of meeting other people and of seeing how they operated. In a club they did work they would not normally do and it was something definite to work to. In the old club they also used to have some very pleasant little outings. They were fortunate in having Mr Gliddon in the town, a great enthusiast and a lantern man. It was agreed to form 'Frome Camera Club' with a subscription of five shillings a year. Professional photographers admitted free. Mr J Bell said it was mostly the maintenance of the dark room which brought the old club into debt, and offered to place at the disposal of members his dark room and his studio for demonstrations occasionally. Those present included: Messrs HA Gliddon, A Greenwell, FC Witham, FH Penny, EE Minns, J Bell, SW Bell, Geo Sudell and FA Vallis Twelve members were enrolled and a provisional committee formed and it was agreed that the Rev HA Hare be invited to be President.

A week later the first general meeting was held in the Temperance Hall and the press reported that '...there was again a most encouraging attendance proving indisputably that the new club was not only needed but that energetic endeavour to supply the want was highly appreciated. The chair was taken by Alan Greenwell and the first business was to consider a report by the provisional committee appointed at the inaugural meeting which principally dealt with a code of rules. The rules were adopted with a few modifications. Mr Gliddon, the Hon Secretary and Treasurer offered a prize of one guinea to the member obtaining the highest number of marks in a monthly competition album. Members could submit entries anonymously and all members invited to vote for what they considered the best entry. The future of the club was discussed and outings and expeditions were provisionally arranged and the first outing was to Vallis Vale on 16 April.

The SS, in reporting the club's first outing to Vallis, said a 'good muster turned out, all bent on making the meeting a success.' Tea was provided by Mrs Williams at the Old Mill House. Members were told by Mr Witham that Mr F Le Gros had authorised him to say that he would be pleased to present a £10 10/- cup to the club, the terms of the competition to be arranged. This was greeted with tremendous applause and a vote of thanks was carried. Mr Le Gros who is a 'skilful photographer,' consented to be a Vice President of the club.

On 18 October a Conversatzione was held at St John's College by invitation of Mr & Mrs Rudd. The room was decorated with plants supplied by Messrs Bourne of Beckington and photographs taken by members decorated the walls. Stereoscopic views were shown and a microscope was available for viewing interesting objects. Photos taken by the x-ray process were also on view and Mr Gliddon gave a lantern lecture. A musical entertainment followed and, at the conclusion, Mr FH Penny proposed a vote of thanks to Mr & Mrs Rudd, seconded by Dr Dalby.

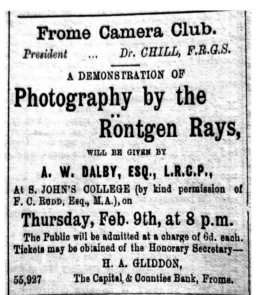

Press Advertisement February 1899

The first lecture in 1899 was in February, the subject being 'Röntgen Rays' by Dr A W Dalby. He used an accumulator to provide the power which passed through an induction coil which consisted of about a mile of fine wire and finally to the bulb. Professor Röntgen discovered the x-ray whilst experimenting with Professor Crook's tubes. It was called an x-ray because no one was able to define it. The x-ray could penetrate flesh but not bones. X-rays were taken of the hands of two of those present, and the plates developed by Mr S Bell, the exposure time being almost four minutes. A foot with the boot on took almost 10 minutes. One or two imperfections in the bones were clearly defined. The x-ray apparatus belonged to the Cottage Hospital.

In March 1899 a large audience attended a lecture at St John's College given by Dr Chill entitled 'Round the World with a Camera.' The tour commenced at Liverpool and visits were made to Canada, USA, Japan, China, Singapore, Ceylon and India returning to

London via the Suez Canal. The localities visited were illustrated by a large number of beautiful views with a powerful lantern. Dr Chill said that, although he always took a camera with him when travelling, the views shown were not his own. Mr Le Gros, in the chair, said that the club had progressed, the summer meetings 'were not altogether such as he would have been glad to have read about.'

Mr Le Gros' comments in referring to what appears to be poor attendance at the first season's summer excursions, was an indication that the initial enthusiasm was rapidly fading. No published accounts of summer visits for the second season of 1899 were found, perhaps because they were poorly attended or cancelled.

Probably the last event in the life of the club was a lecture held at St John's College, given by Mr Gliddon in October 1899. The public were admitted and charged 6d. According to the press report 'very few members of the club or of the general public were present, though the series of excellent slides shown, some by Mr Gliddon, merited better patronage.'

Frome Camera Club experienced a similar fate to the photographic club[1] established in the town a few years earlier which also lasted just two years.

The Somerset Postal Photographic Club 1899-1919

In 1899 Bernard Mitchell of Willow Vale, Frome, inaugurated The Somerset Postal Photographic Club (SPPC). The object of the club was to enable secretaries of camera clubs to circulate to each other by post the work of medal winners in open classes. Clubs using this method mounted the prints in an album and alongside each print was a blank paper for comments. When the album had completed its circulation to members the comments, which were anonymous, were sent to the member who had taken the image. At a house exhibition of the Postal Camera Club held in London in November 1905 Mr J C Warburg said postal clubs had been in existence for twenty years; typically, they included between 12 and 30 members. Some clubs exist for more special and restricted purposes such as architectural detail, hand cameras and clubs for large work. The value of a postal club can hardly be overstated: to see and discuss good prints every month, to have one's own shortcomings pointed out in a friendly way can only be beneficial. There are other advantages of a postal club compared with an exhibition: the prints are looked at separately in the hand or on the desk. They stand on their own merits, uninfluenced by surrounding pictures. We take as much or as little time for each print and do not have to move on before we have finished enjoying a picture because other people are waiting to look at it. The speaker hoped his enthusiasm for portfolio clubs may have helped to convince those present of the very useful gap they fill in photographic matters. There was no quicker or sounder way of developing the artistic side of oneself than to study nature and discuss one's own and other people's pictures. The portfolio clubs are a great help in this.

Mr Mitchell was the Secretary of the SPPC and in 1919 the club celebrated its coming of age by holding a celebration at Bristol. Members came from all parts of the county and from Monmouth, Hereford and Yorkshire. Membership was approximately 60 and about 20 members attended the event. Miss Violet C McAdam of Hereford presented Mr Mitchell with a beautiful bound album containing a photographic print by each member, together with a photograph of the member and their autograph. Mr Edwin Hazell of Cleveland presented Mrs Mitchell with a gold wristlet watch and Mr F J Taylor of Risca (Mon) presented the couple with a silver tea service.

Mr Mitchell held the post of secretary from the club's inception and had only met one of the members prior to the celebration. It is not known for how long the SPPC continued following the 'coming of age' celebrations. Mr Mitchell was also secretary of the Frome Mechanics' Camera Section which was formed in 1902.

Bernard Mitchell died in Frome in 1928 aged 64 and was buried at Downside. He was employed as Company Secretary with E Baily & Sons of Frome.

The Mechanics Institute Camera Club 1902-1906

Yet another camera club venture was formed in Frome, this time by the Mechanics Institute (MI) in 1902, initially it was called a 'Photographic Section.'

An announcement appeared in the press in April stating that it was being started for the instruction of beginners and the improvement of advanced photographers. It would be of general interest in advancing the science and art of photography. There were several advanced photographers in the town who have promised their assistance towards making the new venture a success. Arrangements had been made for the use of a darkroom and from time to time demonstrations would be given in some branch of photography. The public were invited to join by applying to the Secretary of the Photographic Section.

In July the Secretary announced that 15 members had joined and it was proposed to buy 'Amateur Photographer' each week and 'Photographic Art' each month and be made available to members.

In September the MI announced that a three-day Photographic Exhibition and Ping-Pong Tournament would be held in December. The Photographic Exhibition 'would be quite a new feature in the annals of local events.' In November it was announced that the exhibition would be held from 11 to 13 December when large silver and bronze medals and other prizes would be awarded. The exhibition was to be opened by Dr Edwin Chill, the President, and prizes distributed by Mrs Chill. On 5 December the Somerset Standard looked forward to the exhibition where 'some 400 pictures from all parts of the Kingdom and by well-known artists have been entered.'

Dr Chill, in opening the exhibition, was supported on the platform by others including JW Singer. He said they should congratulate the committee on bringing to Frome a collection of photographs that would do credit to a large city. There were 338 entries. One of the judges, Mr JT Ashby FRPS of Loughton, Essex said that 'as an initial effort it is a most remarkably successful display.' The photographs 'showed great promise, many by photographers with less than a year's experience.' He concluded 'your grandly picturesque old town and its beautiful surroundings should afford a profitable hunting ground to the amateur in pictorial photography.' The other judge was Mr Barrow Keane FRPS of Derby. In the Member's Class the following won medals: Bernard Mitchell, JH Wells, Cyril Cuzner, Wilfred L Watson* and George Moore. The Secretary, Mr B Mitchell, in a brief speech said they had made several excursions and held meetings at which practical demonstrations were given. He thought the architectural section was the plum of the exhibition and gave the judges a difficult task. There were many photographers in the town, not members of the society and he hoped that by the annual meeting they would be enrolled. He suggested that the Society might make a pictorial record of all places of note and interest in the town and neighbourhood and that the Urban District Council find accommodation for it.

Andrew Paterson (left) by kind permission of Adrian Harvey, Director of the Andrew Paterson Photographic Collection.

The 2nd Photographic Exhibition arranged by the MI was held in November 1903 over 3 days. The centre of the room, which the previous year had been taken up by Ping-Pong tables was occupied by chairs where visitors watched slides projected on to a screen suspended from the organ gallery. All the slides entered in the competition were shown by CB Bartlett on his projector. At the opening ceremony Dr Chill said that entries had increased despite the entry fee being raised and the exhibition was a great improvement on last year. A new class for slides had been introduced and there were 116 entries. Another innovation was a class for Excursion Prints (for the best print from a negative made on one of the Society's excursions in 1903). The judges were the same as in the previous year. Members awarded medals were as follows: G Moore, H Howell, B J Mitchell, W L Watson, W A King, H E Smith. In the open class for portraits Andrew Paterson of Inverness won a silver medal for a print 'The Plotter.' He established a photographic business when he was 18 years old and gained a distinguished list of clients.

*WL Watson trained as a pharmacist but did not qualify; he opened a drug and photographic shop in Cheap Street in 1902 and published local photographic views. He had a stand of photographic apparatus at the exhibition. He and his wife emigrated to Australia in 1909. He died in Adelaide in 1943. Some of his glass negatives were found in a loft in Ealing in 1989, which are in Frome Museum.

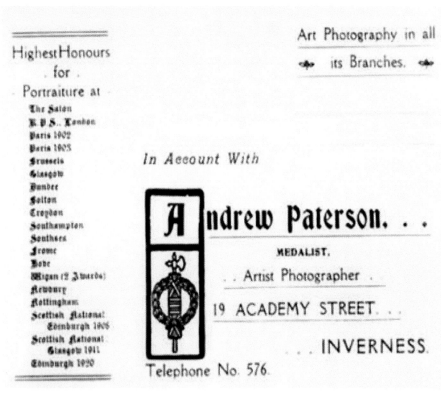

Andrew Paterson's letter heading listing his medal success at Frome.

Bell's Studio, Catherine Street.

Messrs J Bell displayed a collection of their photographs and WL Watson had a display of cameras and photographic equipment. There was also a loan collection of photographs from one of the greatest photographers of the late 19th, early 20th century, Frank M Sutcliffe FRPS of Whitby.

The 3rd exhibition arranged by the MI Photographic Section was held on the 4th to 6th November 1904. Entries were up on the previous year but attendance was down on Saturday due to a performance of The Chinese Honeymoon at the Market Hall. Postcards were introduced as a new class and Cyril Cuzner of Frome won a medal in this class for 'Ladies in Japanese Costume.' In the members' classes, medals were awarded to BJ Mitchell, WA King, H Howell, G Moore. The judges were Mr Barrow Keane FRPS and Mr Frank Sutcliffe FRPS. In the architecture class Mr Mitchell's 'Norman Doorway' (the Ladychapel, Glastonbury Abbey) was 'a splendid bit of work' commented the judges.

Frank Meadow Sutcliffe FRPS, one of the most distinguished photographers of the late 19th and early 20th centuries, famous for his views of Whitby and surrounding area.

The Society became affiliated to the Royal Photographic Society of Great Britain. In 1905 the three-day exhibition was held on 2nd to 4th November. All the slides entered were shown by a limelight lantern and another attraction was a demonstration by the Rotograph Company, an American firm, which produced postcards. On Thursday evening there was a soirée and dance, on Friday, a vocal and instrumental concert and on Saturday, Mr H Grant's Orchestral Band gave a selection of music and humorous songs with WL Watson as MC.

The SS reported that there was a slight reduction in the number of entries and many exhibits were smaller than usual. However, the quality of the exhibits had improved on the previous year. This was particularly evident in the members' classes who had no doubt benefitted from the ideas derived from the open entries at earlier exhibitions. Dr Chill had left the town and Mr AG Hayman was elected president and WL Watson secretary. The judges were the same as the previous year.

In the novices class George Love Dafnis of Bath won a bronze medal for 'The Towpath', a bromide. He later established a photographic business in Bath which continued for many years. Many of his prints taken from glass negatives are available from *Bath in Time.*

Owen Graystone Bird, an accomplished photographer and another Bath entrant, also won medals. He was the son of Frederick Bird[1] who was born in Frome and who established a photographic studio at Dungarvan Buildings, Market Place from 1854 to 1866, when he moved to Bath where he operated a studio in Milsom Street. In a Bath Chronicle advertisement in 1866, he stated that he held a Royal Warrant as photographer to the Prince and Princess of Wales.

In the classes for members and residents of Frome Wilfred L Watson won three medals including one for portraiture: 'The Latest Novel', a bromide. The subject was 'a well-known Horningsham young lady engaged in reading a book by a window.'*
Mr George Moore also won medals. His

Medal awarded to George Love Dafnis in 1905 at the final exhibition at the Mechanics' Institute.

study 'Old Froome' a 'picturesque block of houses at Gorehedge which the Frome Urban Council has seen fit to clear away in the course of the past summer..... is a bit of good honest work,' commented one of the judges. Other local medallists were Bernard J Mitchell and Herbert E Smith.

The MI Photographic Section survived longer than the two earlier attempts at establishing a club for photographers in Frome. The reason for its failure is not known but photography was an expensive hobby: the cost of cameras and glass negatives and the means to develop and print them were beyond the scope of a large section of the population. It is probable that with membership around 20 the numbers were insufficient to sustain a viable club. Another factor may have been that W L Watson, who was one of the leading lights in the group, lost interest when he decided to emigrate to Australia.

* *The archivist at Longleat could not confirm whether she was a member of the Thynne family.*

[1]*ALM, Early Camera Clubs in Frome, FSLS Yearbook 20, 2017*

Sources:
Royal Photographic Society archive.
Local newspapers.

FROME PORTRAITS No 22
Cecil Charles Cole Case (1895-1969)

Picture courtesy of Somerset Cricket Museum

CCC 'Box' Case was born in Frome on 7 September 1895 and was educated at Kings School, Bruton. He served as a second lieutenant in the Third Battalion of the Dorsetshire Regiment throughout the First World War, during which he was wounded at Arras in 1915. He played cricket for Dorset before becoming a regular middle order batsman for Somerset. During his career for Somerset from 1925-35 he scored 8574 runs including nine centuries with a batting average 22.09; he also played twice for the Gentlemen v Players. Once, when facing Richard Tyldesley at Old Trafford, he fell forwards onto the pitch, but still managed to play the ball in front of his forehead. On another occasion, he was confounded by the Nottinghamshire fast bowler, Bill Voce: when diving to avoid a suspected bumper, his wicket was shattered and he picked up a stump, before walking back to the pavilion holding it. Once set, however, he was very difficult to dislodge. He was injured halfway through the 1935 season after which he retired from first class cricket, when Wisden reported: 'If never a stylist, Case could often be relied on to stay a collapse, and for practically half the season his stubborn tactics were much missed.' Another commentator wrote that he was 'the grimmest batsman he had ever seen.' Cecil Case was a member of the family which owned the Tannery[1] at Keyford. He was a bachelor and died at 'The Limes' at the corner of Stevens Lane and Keyford on 11 November 1969 aged 74.

[1]*Frome Buildings No 20, FSLS Yearbook 20, 2017*
My thanks to Gerald Quartley for information on Cecil 'Box' Case. Ed

Locomotive Frome

L & S.W. Railway locomotive 'Frome' no 114, Yeovil Town station c 1860

Written on the back of a copy of this image is the following: "One of the first passenger engines employed at the Yeovil Town Station. Original photograph taken c1860-1. On the foot plate are the driver, John Knight, who later became the licensee of the Half Moon Hotel. Matthew Woods (centre figure) the loco foreman and William Greenaway, Fireman. William Dyer (not in the Picture) was the cleaner. He eventually became a driver and died in Yeovil in 1922. This photograph is a rarity as the Driver who had the photograph taken had used the company's coal, oil and engine on a Sunday to have the photograph taken. When found out, he was taken up to Nine Elm's Shed and severely reprimanded. He was then told to hand over all photographs and copies to be destroyed. This one, however, escaped, as did the original negative.

Image and information courtesy of Community Heritage Access Centre, Yeovil, (01935) 462886 heritage.services@southsomerset.gov.uk
Website: www.southsomersetheritage.org.uk

Frome in Palestine 1917 – 1948
The Story of an Exhibition
by Adam Stout

'Frome in Palestine 1917 - 1948' was the title of an exhibition held at the Silk Mill in Frome from 18-31 October, 2017. It was the culmination of a long-term project by Frome Friends of Palestine to mark the centenary of the Balfour Declaration and General Allenby's march on Jerusalem in 1917. To some, the annexation of Palestine seemed like the culmination of a dream, but Britain's thirty-year rule of Palestine rapidly became a nightmare, conflicting and contradictory promises were made to both Arabs and Jews. In November 1917, the British Foreign Secretary, Arthur Balfour pledged to create 'a national home for the Jewish people in Palestine, it being clearly understood that nothing shall be done which may prejudice the civil and religious rights of the existing non-Jewish communities in Palestine.' The so-called Balfour Declaration was to have profound and lasting effects.

Large numbers of people took part in Britain's Palestine experience. Some came from Frome; others had descendants who now live in Frome. The exhibition was designed to ground this conflict by telling the story of the town's connection with Palestine, from the heady days of the Palestine Exploration Fund, through the era of religious enthusiasts, refugees and tourists, the soldiers who served and sometimes died in the Great War, to public servants and policemen caught in a conflict not of their own making, who tried to make the Mandate work.

It was not an easy exhibition, but Britain's time in Palestine is not an easy subject. By putting Frome people at the heart of it, we sought to acknowledge their often-forgotten contribution, and to help local people today get a better sense of the roots of the conflict in the much-abused Holy Land.

In addition to the exhibition itself, we had two computer monitors with a range of relevant videos, including the Balfour Project's 'Britain in Palestine 1917-1948', a short but excellent introduction to the situation; a compilation of clips from old newsreel and documentaries put together by members of the group, recent footage taken by a local human rights observer, and a powerful and impassioned monologue by Holly Law, then 18, who went to Bi'lin in her gap year; we also put on a series of events. The exhibition was formally opened by Raymond Asquith, Lord Oxford, at a packed evening event, followed by a talk from Dr Peter Shambrook, a historian and an expert on the background to the Balfour Declaration. With the producer's blessing, we screened Peter Kosminsky's gripping four-part docu-drama *The Promise* over two consecutive nights.

Inside the Exhibition

Objects bring the past to life, and several local people trusted us to display family heirlooms and memorabilia. Letters, photographs, medals, a mother-of-pearl Palestine Police sweetheart brooch, a Turkish bayonet brought back from Palestine after the Great

War and later used for spearing farm-rats, signed copies of Israel Zangwill's books, amongst many other curious items. The heart of the exhibition was the sequence of twenty 'Britain in Palestine' background boards, nailed to battens along the gallery walls, and sixteen 'Frome in Palestine' boards, which were mounted back-to-back across two sets of ingenious folding screens, kindly lent to us by Holy Trinity church.

The exhibition

The first boards set the scene. The word Palestine, derived from 'Philistine', was in use both before and during the long period under Ottoman rule. Although the population was overwhelmingly Moslem, there were sizeable and well-integrated Christian and Jewish communities, which in 1914 accounted for 11% and 5% of the population respectively. Palestine was an important exporter of agricultural products such as soap, wine and cotton, as well as Jaffa oranges, and barley was grown for the British brewing industry.

Seen as the Holy Land for all three Abrahamic religions, there was a growing Christian tourism industry in the 19th century, and marked competition between European countries to establish their own churches there. Driven by a combination of colonial and religious zeal, organisations such as the Palestine Exploration Fund mapped and charted the Holy Land, and their attractive maps demonstrated that Palestine was a well-settled and prosperous place, but, as happened elsewhere in the British Empire, the existence of the 'native' population was ignored by some at home. Christian Zionists such as Lord Shaftesbury urged the settlement of Jews in Palestine in the belief that encouraging their 'return' to the land they had occupied in Biblical times would hasten their conversion to Christianity.

Moslems, Jews and Orthodox Christians at a religious festival outside the
Damascus Gates of Jerusalem, c1900
Picture:Eric and Edith Matson Photograph Collection

During the 19th century, Britain had generally been supportive of the Ottoman Empire, sometimes labelled 'the sick man of Europe' because of its inability to resist the depredations of its more powerful neighbours, however, in 1914 the Ottomans sided with Germany, which therefore made them Britain's enemies. An Ottoman attack on the Suez Canal was repelled by British forces, which then moved northwards and entered Palestine in the spring of 1917. Two attempts to take Gaza were repelled by the Ottomans, but under the new command of General Allenby in November British forces finally took control of southern Palestine. The British capture of Jerusalem on 9 December 1917 was hailed in Britain as a symbolic victory for a Christian nation, but there were still many months of hard fighting before the Ottoman forces were driven out of Palestine in October 1918.

In order to win support for the war effort, the British made three contradictory promises. They encouraged the ambitions of Hussein, Sharif of Mecca, who was promised a kingdom if he took a major part in an insurrection against the Turks: this was the campaign in which T E Lawrence 'of Arabia' took part. But at the same time, Britain and France were planning a carve-up of the Ottoman Empire (the Sykes-Picot Agreement) which left little room for an independent Arab kingdom, and on 2 November 1917, encouraged by the aspirations of the World Zionist Federation and a belief that supporting Zionism would bring America into the War, the British Foreign Secretary Arthur Balfour made his now-notorious 'Balfour Declaration' in a letter to the Zionist leader Lord Rothschild:

His Majesty's government view with favour the establishment in Palestine of a national home for the Jewish people, and will use their best endeavours to facilitate the achievement of this object, it being clearly understood that nothing shall be done which may prejudice the civil and religious rights of existing non-Jewish communities in Palestine, or the rights and political status enjoyed by Jews in any other country.

Even amongst British Jews, this was a very controversial statement. Many were bitterly opposed to the idea of creating a Jewish 'homeland' in another country since they saw this as undermining their own hard-won civil rights in this one. Edwin Montagu, the only Jewish member of Lloyd George's cabinet, even suggested that the Zionist organisation should be 'proscribed .... as illegal and against the national interest.' [1]

Once the War was over, Britain and France specifically excluded Palestine from plans to restore Arab rule to Arab countries. In the words of Arthur Balfour, 'in Palestine we do not propose even to go through the form of consulting the wishes of the present inhabitants of the country.'[2] In 1923, Britain's occupation of Palestine was recognised by the newly-formed League of Nations, which granted Britain a formal mandate to govern Palestine. The Mandate placed much emphasis on encouraging Jewish immigration and the mechanics of creating a Jewish homeland, but the rights of the existing Arab population were not mentioned at all. The Jewish homeland prospered; it was more or less self-governing, well-organised and well-funded, and during the 1920s about 100,000 Jews, mostly from eastern Europe, came to Palestine. The Arab majority, however, were ruled as a Crown colony, and rights to self-government were denied because of Arab opposition to the Balfour Declaration. As Winston Churchill, then Colonial Secretary, explained 'No representative bodies that may be established will be permitted to interfere with measures (e.g. immigration etc) designed to give effect to the principle of a National Home or to challenge this principle.' [3]

Arab anger erupted into violence in August 1929. British troops struggled to restore order, and the Government belatedly acknowledged that it had equal obligations to Arabs as well as to Jews. The Passfield White Paper of October 1930 recommended limitations on land sales and Jewish immigration to Palestine. However, following criticism from Zionist supporters in the British parliament, the Paper was discarded by Prime Minister Ramsay MacDonald. Jewish immigration increased dramatically during the 1930s as a result of Nazi oppression in Germany and elsewhere in Europe, a problem exacerbated by the refusal of countries such as Britain and the US to open their own borders to Jewish refugees. The result in Palestine was a three-year rebellion, between 1936 and 1939, which was brutally suppressed. Collective punishment, wholesale destruction of villages, human shields, reprisals, detention camps, and other policies that many today associate with Israel, were first used in Palestine by British troops.

Lord Balfour's visit to Palestine to open the Hebrew University at Jerusalem, April 1925.

In 1939, with world war once more looming and the Palestinians militarily defeated, the British produced another White Paper which proposed limiting Jewish immigration and eventually setting up a power-sharing arrangement. The Jewish population reacted with a series of protests and the formation of underground terrorist organisations such as the Irgun, which during and after the end of the War organised a series of high-profile attacks on symbols of British power designed to force them out of the country. The best known of these was the bombing of the King David Hotel in 1946. It was the seat of the British administration, and 91 people were killed. Although enormous numbers of British police and service personnel were recruited, the situation was out of control, and a bankrupt Britain was under increasing pressure from America to support the claims of the Zionists. Proposals to partition Palestine, drawn up by the newly-formed UN, were angrily rejected by both sides. In 1947 the British declared that the Mandate would end on 15 May 1948, and on that day they left, abandoning the Palestinian population to its fate.

The Frome Connection

Jane Daniel of Nunney Court
Picture: Visit Nunney

The second part of the exhibition dealt with Frome's own connections with Palestine, beginning with the keen interest local people took in the Holy Land during the 19th century. A lively local branch of the Palestine Exploration Fund was set up in 1869. The Reverend Alfred Daniel, vicar of Holy Trinity, was the first secretary, and in 1902 his daughter-in-law Jane went on tour to Palestine. Her diary is full of interesting observations about the country at that time, which thanks to the generosity of her grandson Hilary Daniel, we were able to put on display. Amongst the people Jane Daniel visited was George Blyth, Anglican Bishop of Jerusalem from 1886, whose great-grand-daughter and biographer Ann Phillips lives in Frome. Energetic and keen, Blyth raised money for many projects across his huge diocese, including the new St George's Cathedral in Jerusalem.

Several local people have Jewish ancestors who were involved in early Jewish projects to settle Palestine. Roger Birnstingl's grandparents Avigdor and Cordelia Birnstingl took part in the 'Maccabean Pilgrimage' from London to Palestine, organised in 1897 on a lavish scale by the writer Israel Zangwill and the lawyer Herbert Bentwich, whose great-niece Juliet Solomon lives in Frome. Elaine Pugsley's grandparents were amongst the many Jews who fled persecution in Russia and went to Palestine. They met in Jaffa in 1912, and married there, but two years later, after war broke out, left for Egypt on the advice of the British and settled in London after the war ended.

Many local people went to Palestine during the Great War. The Somerset Light Infantry took part in the British invasion of 1917, and many Frome soldiers fought with them. Two attacks on Gaza were repelled with heavy loss of life, and six months of stalemate and trench warfare ensued.

The Maccabean Pilgrimage, 1897   *Picture: Roger Birnstingl*

Two Frome soldiers have left us graphic accounts of the Second Battle of Gaza. Tank commander, Lieutenant Maurice Shore of Whatley House, was awarded the Military Cross for showing 'great daring and gallantry' in command of his tank. 'Although wounded, he continued to fight his tank until all his gunners were put out of action.' A long letter from Corporal Frank Phillips, who'd worked for Butler & Tanner before the war, was published in the *Somerset Standard* on 16 November 1917, but he was already dead, killed by a direct hit from a shell, before publication.

Several other Frome soldiers lost their lives during the Palestine campaign. Private Herbert Speller, of Christchurch St East, who had worked for the Lamb Brewery at Gorehedge, died from wounds received whilst digging trenches near Gaza. Two Captains were wounded by a shell just five miles short of Jerusalem, and died later: Edward Harford, the son of the late vicar of Marston Bigot, and Adam Bealey, President of the Frome Conservative Club. Privates George Cooper, chauffeur to the vicar of East Woodlands, and Victor Slade, of The Butts, were both killed in action. The body of Private Wyndham Hames, a Mells gamekeeper, was only found six months after he had been killed. Second-Lieutenant George Wheeler, from Somerset Road, served all over Palestine before joining the RAF; he was killed in a flying accident in Egypt.

Many made it home again, of course. People like Fritz George, who before the war had worked for a baker in Catherine Hill, joined the Army Service Corps as a field baker, served in Palestine where he acquired a lifelong dislike of sand. Captain Cecil Ames, son of Herbert Ames, senior partner in the solicitors' firm of Ames Kent, went on to become a distinguished judge. Lieutenant Ronald Vallis became a well-known local architect.

Ann Phillips at St George's Anglican Cathedral, Jerusalem
Picture: Ann Phillips

Ann Phillips' grandfather, John Bernard Barron, was an important figure in the civil administration set up after the war was over. Appointed Deputy Military Governor in Jericho in April 1918, he later became Director of Customs and Revenue. He was Superintendent of Palestine's first full census in 1922, an enormous and controversial project, and was also tasked with sorting out the finances of the impoverished Orthodox Church. He resigned at the end of March 1924, one of several senior British officials to leave in protest at what was seen as High Commissioner Herbert Samuel's pro-Zionist policies. One newspaper described it as 'The New Exodus'.

The escalation of violence in the 1930s and 1940s led to a huge expansion in the numbers of people serving in the military and in the Palestine Police. By the end of 1946 Britain had 16,000 British and local police and more than 100,000 British troops stationed in Palestine. They came from every part of the country, and some of them came from Frome. Len Pearce of Badcox enlisted in the Palestine Police in 1943. He served as armed escort to the High Commissioner and was sent on some secret and highly-sensitive missions, and on one occasion escorted Sir Winston Churchill's daughter, Sarah, to the Sea of Galilee. His friend Ken Dayman-Johns was a military Despatch Rider, who in later life had many stories of his wartime experiences to tell his children in Nunney. John Bedford's father, John Bedford senior, had left home when John was only a baby, but we do know that he served with the Palestine Police and was mentioned in despatches. By contrast Michael Hobbs' father, Herbert, kept all of his Palestine Police papers, which he kindly allowed us to put on display.

Julian Asquith, Lord Oxford from Mells, became Assistant District Commissioner in Gaza and Beersheba, an area which included the desert home of most of Palestine's Bedouin population, and is remembered as having done much to assist them. In 1945 he became private secretary to the last High Commissioner of Palestine. He left the country on the last day. 'Many of us at the time thought it wrong to have relinquished our responsibilities in the way we did and to relinquish them when the consequences were so foreseeable', he told the House of Lords years later.[4]

The Only Way to Peace

This was the title of the last board in the exhibition. Since Israel annexed the rest of Mandate Palestine following the Six Day War in 1967, it has been steadily taking over Palestinian land and villages. There are now 600,000 Israeli citizens living in illegal settlements in the Occupied Territories. But Palestine's people are not disappearing with their lands. Their numbers are increasing, and now, for the first time since 1949, there are as many Palestinians as Israelis. The Palestinian population is set to outstrip the number of Israelis by 2020. Some Israeli commentators call this the 'demographic timebomb'. The peoples of historic Palestine have no choice but to live together. Britain has a special responsibility for what is happening in Israel/Palestine. Robert Cohen, a Jewish commentator, has proposed the following updated version of the Balfour Declaration as the starting-point for a new approach. At 67 words, it is exactly the same length as the original:

Julian Asquith, Lord Oxford, Assistant District Commissioner at Beersheba
Picture: Raymond Asquith

Her Majesty's government view with favour the establishment in Israel/Palestine of a safe and secure home for all who live there. The nations of the world should use their best endeavours to facilitate the achievement of this objective, it being clearly understood that nothing shall be done which may prejudice the civil, political and religious rights of Jews or Palestinians living in Israel/Palestine or any other country.

What could be fairer than that?

[1] *ES Montagu, Memorandum on the Anti-Semitism of the Present Government, August 1917*
[2] *Arthur Balfour, Memorandum to Lord Curzon, 11 August 1917*
[3] *Winston Churchill to High Commissioner Herbert Samuel, 21 June 1921*
[4] *Hansard, 26 May 1982, vol 430*

Details of the full exhibition are available online at https://fromeinpalestineexhibition2017.wordpress.com and more information about planning the exhibition can be obtained by contacting the author through info@fsls.org.uk

TO AUTHORS AND PUBLISHERS.

Publications will be impartially reviewed by us if left at Mr. C. A. Bartlett's, 32, Paternoster Row, London, addressed to " Mr. A. Byrt, High Street, Shepton Mallet," or forwarded at once to our office.

"AN OUTSTRETCHED HAND TO THE FALLEN."— (By Mrs. G. W. Sheppard.)—Six-pence per dozen. Penny, Frome.—This pamphlet is a plain sketch of the labours of its truly excellent writer in the town of Frome. For years past her sympathies have been drawn out on behalf of the fallen sisterhood: and those who will read her previous work—" Sunshine in the Workhouse"—may ascertain how Mrs. Sheppard acquired an insight into their too real miseries. She now tells us what she has effected and hopes to effect towards a permanent refuge in Frome. A house rented at £6 per annum, and furnished second-hand for £20 is presided over by a reliable old woman, and already six or eight poor girls are admitted and full of gratitude to their lady visitor. Mrs. Sheppard appeals thus for christian aid :—" I have only funds sufficient to take me over Christmas. Must I give it up then ? Remember you have no machinery of committees, salaries, printed reports, &c., to support. My old woman is contented with her house, rent free, fire and food. So any donations would be appropriated at once to the object I have in view. Help me to enlarge my refuge and win more in, or else work out the same plan *in your own town ;* but don't leave these, our un-fortunate sisters, without words of kindness to welcome them back to the paths of virtue and womanly happiness and peace with God."

Thanks to ALM for this extract from the Shepton Mallet Journal, 1859. Nick Hersey described Emma Sheppard's 'Small Deeds of Kindness' in FSLS Yearbook 20, 2017

Goose Marsh Mill, West Woodlands, Frome
by James Richardson

Located in the corner of Mill Piece Field on former Longleat estate land in the village of West Woodlands are the ruins of Goose Marsh Mill. The site today contains the ruins, the water wheel pit, dam wall, drained pond and tail leat outlet. The ruins which are clearly visible from the B3092 at West Woodlands are composed of the original western wall of the mill with later and currently roofless, lean-to extensions and the severely truncated north wall which is reduced to approx 1 ¾ storey height. The inner area of the mill is now mainly occupied by some concrete block pig styes and a much later corrugated iron building. The tail leat outlet is a small stone arch located in the stream bank directly in line with the wheel pit. Some limited excavations have also revealed the north western footings adjacent to the wheel pit. Now breached on the line of the stream, the dam wall is of similar construction to the mill building with supporting earth bank. The outline of the drained pond is distinct.

Having bought the fields and ruins in 2016, I was interested to find out more about them. An excellent starting point was the *Industries of Frome* by Rodney Goodall[1], which gave some information on the mill (interchangeably named West Woodlands Mill and Goose Marsh Mill in some texts) and its change of use over the years. The *Industries of Frome* led me to Alastair MacLeay and Michael McGarvie who kindly arranged for a site visit by Ken Rogers. Subsequent map research and the excellent Longleat estate archive House Historian research service revealed much fascinating initial information about Goose Marsh Mill[2] and its tenants. This article gives a brief summary of the history of the mill from the late 18th century to the present day.

The earliest records with a direct link to the mill show that the land on which it now stands was leased from Longleat to a James Jesser in 1744 and had been held by that family since at least 1656. Jesser family members included cordwainers and clothiers through the 17th and 18th centuries so the land's connection with the textile industry predates the present mill.

On 15 September 1794 a new lease was granted to the millwright William Jesser which describes the future site of the mill as, 'A messuage or dwelling house with outhouses, buildings, garden and orchard.' Today nothing remains of this original property other than its boundary hedge and a flat area which indicates where the house once stood. With the security of a new lease, it appears that between 1794 and 1798 William Jesser initiated the development of the site. A subsequent lease of 1815 to a George Kingdon describes the site as including a, 'Mill for machinery and Clothiers Workshops lately erected and built by John Ayres.' An indistinct pencil note in the records suggests the mill was built 17 years previously which would put the build date around 1798. According to *Wiltshire and Somerset Woollen Mills[3]*, Ayres was a leaseholder of the mill, presumably sublet from William Jesser.

The mention of clothier's workshops makes clear Goose Marsh was a textile mill but no information on the mill's specific purpose has yet been discovered. If it was a fulling mill, that would probably have been mentioned in the lease so its purpose must have been to house powered textile equipment. The date of the building suggests the mill contained water powered spinning machines (water frames) which produced yarn which would then be put out to the handloom weavers in the Frome area.

The mill seems to have continued as a textile mill up to a date prior to 1831 when it appears in a list of water powered mills annotated as a corn mill. This accords with the general historical narrative as by that stage the Somerset woollen industry was being eclipsed by that of Yorkshire; so many small textile premises were repurposed as they were uncompetitive in their original use. In 1847 the tenancy of the mill was taken by Joseph Seer and the lease changed to rack rent. This meant that the tenant paid a much-increased annual rent but responsibility for maintaining the mill became the landlord's. Prior to that the tenant paid very little rent but was responsible for repairs to the property. From that date details of repairs to the mill appear in the Longleat archives, for example, in 1851 a blacksmith carried out repairs to the water wheel, two years later the hatchways (part of the sluices) were repaired and in 1860 new windows and doors were fitted.

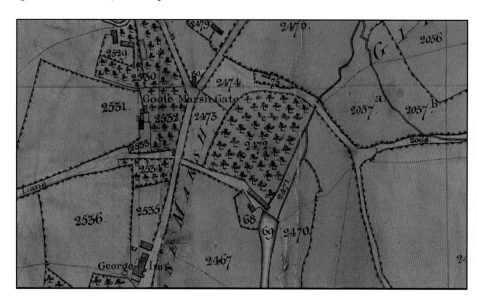

The 1813 Cruse Map[4] showing the original dwelling house (68), immediately to the north is the mill with the pond (69) to the south. Battle Farm (2529) was the scene of the murder of Sarah Watts[5] in 1854

After 1853 the original house mentioned in the 1794 lease was demolished as it does not appear on the 1860 map which also shows the addition of the two lean-to buildings, the remains of which can still be seen. However, the remains do suggest the extensions were quite cheaply built as they are not keyed into the original structure and have suffered significant movement whereas the remaining original mill walls are still perfectly straight.

Ruins of the North wall

Ruins of the Western wall and lean-to buildings

From the 1860s it appears the central section of the mill was converted to a dwelling house with the western lean-to extensions and eastern sections remaining as commercial property. The different sections of the mill can be seen in the map below.

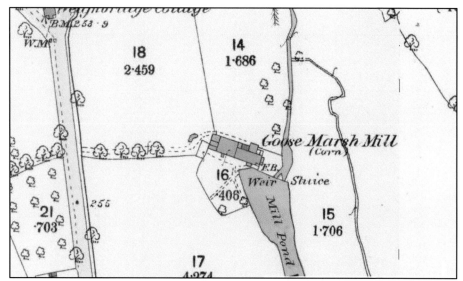

OS Map 25" of the 1841-1952 series[6] shows the most detailed plan of the mill found to date. The ruins which can be seen from the B3092 are the lean-to extension on the western end of the mill, divided into three parts

George Seer seems to have been the last resident of the dwelling house at Goose Marsh Mill. He was granted leave to occupy the house rent free for the rest of his life in September 1902 but died less than two months later. By 1904 the house was noted to be ruinous. The house, buildings and associated lands were sold by Longleat on 29 September 1920. The conveyance papers suggest that by this date, although part of the buildings at Goose Marsh were still standing, most of the structures connected to the former industry at the site were redundant, the house 'ruinous', the sluice 'allowed to go down', and the weir 'now dry and cultivated partly as a garden'.

After 1920 the remaining parts of the mill were used for agricultural purposes. At some point a set of pig styes was built in the space previously occupied by the western end of the dwelling house. The western lean-to extensions were used to keep cattle, most recently by the Williams family who are well known Frome butchers and farmers. In the late 1980s the pigs and cattle were no longer kept at the mill site and the buildings were disused. By the early 21st century, the roof had fallen in and the leans-to extensions' walls were leaning severely.

An interesting find by a metal detectorist in 2017 was a large steel key, about $5^{1}/_{2}$ inches long, which was buried in the field just to the west of the mill. While it may be a coincidence I like to think this is the key to Goose Marsh Mill once in the hand of William Jesser and his successors!

The site is now home to the free range egg producer, Frome Eggs. Work on excavating the wheel pit and the foundations of the eastern end of the mill has begun, as has work to stabilise the remaining structure. The pre-1794 house made itself felt when a planned orchard had to be relocated as it was impossible to dig through the remaining rubble.

Goose Marsh Mill and its site have seen many changes since 1798; it has been a fascinating project to start investigating its history. I feel there is still much to be discovered and look forward to further investigations. If any readers have any more information on the mill or its tenants it would be gratefully received; please contact the author via info@fsls.org.uk

[1]*Goodall RD, The Industries of Frome, FSLS, 2009*
[2]*Longleat Enterprises, Goose Marsh Mill, West Woodlands, 2018, private communication*
[3]*Rogers KH, Wiltshire and Somerset Woollen Mills, Pasold Research Fund, 1976*
[4]*Jeremiah* Cruse, *A map of the Parish of Frome Selwood in the county of Somerset, 1813*
[5]*Davis M & Lassman D, The awful Killing of Sarah Watts, Pen and Sword, 2018*
[6]http://maps.nls.uk/geo/explore/#zoom=18&lat=51.1970&lon=-2.3203&layers=178&b=1

Other maps consulted
OS Map Somerset XLIII.SW 6", *1885,* http://maps.nls.uk
OS Map Somerset XLIII.NW 6", *1885,* http://maps.nls.uk
OS Map Somerset XLIII.SW 6", *1904,* http://maps.nls.uk
OS Map Sheet 166 Frome, 1" to Mile, 7th Series 1952-1961, 1*959,* http://maps.nls.uk

FROME BUILDINGS No 22
Zion Congregational Chapel

The original Zion Chapel was on the site of the octagonal Sunday School at the bottom of Chapel Barton and was occupied by a group of Moravians in the 1770s. In time they were joined by a new congregation which outgrew the building and a chapel was built with approaches from Whittox Lane and Chapel Barton. It was opened in July 1810. Cottages which stood in front of the Chapel in Whittox Lane were removed in 1818, while the old chapel which had served as a schoolroom was taken down and the land converted to a cemetery. In 1888, the Chapel was renovated both inside and out; cottages on each side of the Chapel were demolished to make a better approach and a striking Italianate facade, designed and built by Joseph Chapman jr was added onto the western front which remains impressive today. During the late 19th century, Zion Congregational Chapel was the favoured church of many influential industrialists and local politicians such as John Sinkins, Joseph Tanner, Philip LeGros, Samuel and Henry Rawlings, Joseph Chapman jr, Edward Flatman etc.

Following the closure of Rook Lane Chapel in 1968, the two congregations were due to combine, although some members preferred not to join the United Reformed Church as Zion had become. Zion Congregational Chapel finally closed in 2015 and has been restored as a popular community centre.

I am indebted to Gerald Quartley for the lithograph of Zion Chapel, as it was originally built in 1810. Ed

The Bushes, their Family and Professional Network
by David Smart

Dr Edwin Bush

Dr Edwin Bush (1807-79) featured as the 'Frome Portrait' in Frome Society Yearbook 20[1]. It was stated that he lived in Gentle Street in the house formerly belonging to Dr Francis Bush and the latter's son Dr Francis John Bush, but that he was not related to them. This is not quite correct. Members of the Bush family held positions as medical, legal and clerical professionals for several generations in and around Frome. They intermarried with similar families, some of them very wealthy, including Bushes from Ilminster, near Chard. Many of them and their relatives are memorialised in wall tablets at St John's Church.

Francis Bush (c1776-1843)

Francis Bush was a well-respected figure in Frome. His memorial tablet tells us that he was 'For 46 years, a surgeon in this town. In his profession he was skilful, kind, and unwearied; the esteem in which he was held, and the regret caused by his death was testified on the day of his interment when more than 400 persons followed his remains to the grave.' This esteem stood Francis in good stead in 1829, when Charles Oldfield brought a lawsuit against him, accusing Francis of engaging in criminal conversation with his wife while treating her. A maidservant gave graphic evidence of hearing talking and kissing as she listened at the parlour door, but the plea was dismissed and Bush's character 'rescued from all suspicion.'

Lucretia Dorothy Edgell (c1764-1842)

Francis must already have enjoyed high regard as a young man to marry Lucretia Dorothy Edgell after the death of her first husband, Lieut John Jones. Lucretia was the eldest daughter of Chaffin Edgell, who was born in Standerwick Court and subsequently lived in Keyford House and in Clifton. Her mother was descended from the Folkes family of Norfolk; her brother Harry Edgell and his son Harry were to become Admirals; another brother, Edward, married into the Wickham clerical and legal dynasty and became Rector of Rodden and Prebendary of Wells. Lucretia's great grandfather, James Edgell (c1659-1729), was on close terms with local clothier families, such as the Smiths. He left £1,500 a year to his daughter Ann providing she married a man with an income of £3,000, stipulating that an ecclesiastical benefice would not count. He made a bequest of legal tomes which, he asserted, were 'worth more than £1,000 to a man who hath a ground fit for the study and practice of the law and will to applye himself so as to be eminent in it.' Six poor old men of Standerwick were to carry his body to be buried at Beckington church, each receiving a hat, black coat and stockings for the occasion. A 'plain' marble tablet was to be set up with a [mis]quotation from Horace: *Vir bonus est quis lui consulta patrum qui legis juraque servat.* (A good man is one who takes the advice of the elders, who serves the law and justice.)

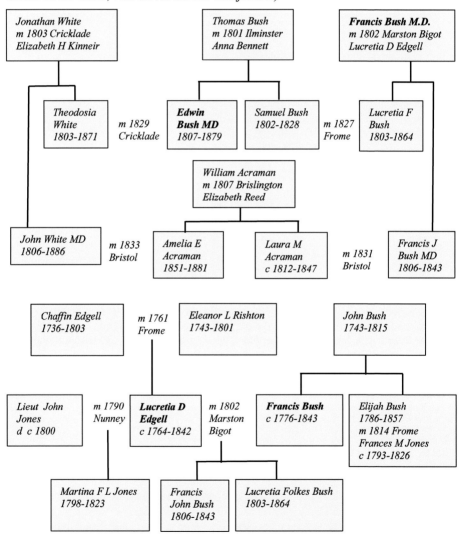

John Bush (1743-1815), father of Francis

Although Francis Bush was buried, married and had both his children baptised in Anglican churches, he regularly appears as a witness to nonconformist births registered at Dr Williams' Library. There is no record for his own birth around 1776, though his parents subsequently baptised their children at All Saints, Farmborough, and were buried there themselves.

Francis's father, John Bush, was probably baptised in Kilmersdon in 1743. Francis and his older brother John may have been sons of their father's first wife, Betty Cradock: two sons by his second wife Hannah were given 'Cradock' as a second forename. By 1779 the family were living in Farmborough and subsequently in Twerton, nearer Bath. In a notice in the Bath Chronicle in 1792 headed 'Cancers cured without incision,' John announced his move and readiness to attend those afflicted with all 'Scrophulous Humours etc' and 'likewise in Midwifery.' He claimed to have cured 'many persons… deemed incurable by the most eminent of the faculty in this kingdom,' assuring prospective patients that they would be treated 'with the utmost candour and sincerity' and 'the greatest tenderness and humanity.' Newspapers in this period are peppered with claims for patent medicines. In *Middlemarch*, set around 1830, George Eliot chronicles the young and ambitious Doctor Lydgate's struggles with the existing healthcare providers, some of whom he regards as mercenary quacks. It was only in 1743 that the Company of Surgeons broke away from the Barber-Surgeons; it received a royal charter in 1800, becoming the Royal College of Surgeons in London and, in 1843, the Royal College of Surgeons of England. On qualifying as surgeons, doctors referred to themselves as 'Mr' to distinguish themselves from mere physicians.

Elijah Bush (1786-1857) and the family he married into

John Bush's practice prospered in Bath, judging by his will. This was proved in the Prerogative Court of Canterbury by Elijah Bush, a son by his second marriage. Elijah practised as a solicitor in Trowbridge, and he witnessed and proved the wills of several of his Somerset cousins. Two of these, sons of his uncle James of Radstock, served as army surgeons. Elijah, and his namesake cousin Elijah both appear as executors in the 1826 will of George Bush of the 6th Regiment of Foot. Elijah, son of John, married Frances Maria Jones at St John's in 1814. She seems to have been part of the Frome circle in which Elijah's brother, Francis, moved.

Dorothy Church, née Rishton (c1744-1825)

There is another tablet in St John's to the memory of 'Mrs Dorothy Church, of this town, (Widow of Captain John Church… only Sister of Eleanor Lucretia wife of the late Chaffin Edgell Esqr and the last surviving grand-daughter of Martin Folkes, Esqr, President of the Royal Society,)…' After the death of Samuel Jesser, her first husband, Dorothy Rishton married John Church of Coleraine, but had no children by either marriage. As sister of Eleanor Lucretia Edgell, she was the aunt by marriage of Francis

Bush. Dorothy named Elijah Bush as one of the trustees and executors of her will, leaving him a leasehold house in Bristol for himself and £1,000, the interest of which was to be paid to his wife Frances Maria Bush, 'my adopted child and Goddaughter,' and to their children after Frances died. Dorothy left appreciable sums to nieces and nephews, adding 18 codicils to her will in the last five years of her life. Most of these are little keepsakes, but three are of a different nature. A few months after signing her will Dorothy declared, 'I have experienced such unkind and improper conduct from Lucretia Dorothy Bush my niece as to determine me no longer to acknowledge her and particularly on a late occasion upon which I have been grossly insulted by her husband.' She revoked all bequests to her niece, 'it being my sense and opinion of her conduct that she hath justly forfeited all claim to friendship and regard.' The legacies went instead to Dorothy's nephew Richard Edgell, a surgeon in Bristol. In another codicil, Martin(a) Lucretia Folkes Jones, daughter of Dorothy's niece Lucretia Dorothy by her marriage to Lieut Jones, had a £500 bequest reduced to £400, 'in consequence of her total neglect of me and giving up her best friend and relation for a total stranger.' It was restored after a couple of weeks, but 'poor dear Martin Jones' died that summer, aged 25.

Dorothy had left £100 to her friend Alicia, widow of William Ireland, vicar of Frome, but revoked this in the wake of the controversies over Rev Stephen Hyde Cassan[2], 'as she has thought proper to drop my acquaintance on account of my not choosing to become a party in her quarrel with her daughter, Mrs Cassan.' The daughter was made beneficiary in place of her mother.

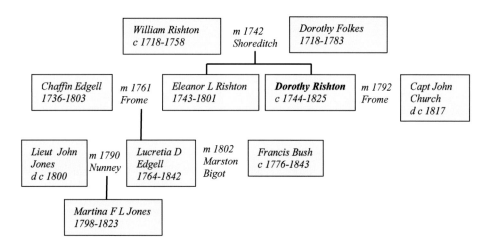

Elijah Bush's family

Elijah and his wife Frances Maria gave their four children family names. Their eldest son, John Jones Bush, became a solicitor, like his father. The two daughters were given 'Rishton' as a middle name; Dorothy married a vicar and Frances a surgeon. Their younger brother, Martin Folkes Bush, practised as a surgeon in Corsham; he married a younger sister of his brother John's wife Hannah Collins. Elijah's wife Frances died at 33, however, leaving four children less than ten years old. We can only wonder who cared for them during the fifteen years before Elijah remarried, to Mary Collins of Stanton Drew. There was much intermarriage between Bushes and Collinses in this part of the country: Elijah's wife Mary was originally from Timsbury, and her mother Elizabeth was a Bush: Elijah and Mary may have been cousins.

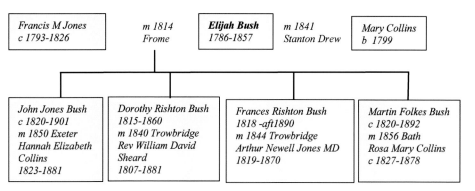

Francis M Jones c 1793-1826	m 1814 Frome	**Elijah Bush** 1786-1857	m 1841 Stanton Drew	Mary Collins b 1799

John Jones Bush c 1820-1901 m 1850 Exeter Hannah Elizabeth Collins 1823-1881	Dorothy Rishton Bush 1815-1860 m 1840 Trowbridge Rev William David Sheard 1807-1881	Frances Rishton Bush 1818 -aft1890 m 1844 Trowbridge Arthur Newell Jones MD 1819-1870	Martin Folkes Bush c 1820-1892 m 1856 Bath Rosa Mary Collins c 1827-1878

Francis Bush's family

Memorials in St John's Church

In addition to Lucretia's daughter by her first marriage, Martina Folkes Lucretia Jones, she had a daughter Lucretia Folkes Bush and a son Francis John Bush who became a surgeon like his father, but was to outlive him by only seven weeks. In 1831 Francis John married Laura Matilda Acraman, daughter of a wealthy Bristol merchant, three of whose four daughters married surgeons.

Francis John and Laura Matilda's son, Francis Acraman Bush, was set to study under a surgeon, but instead lived off his inheritance. He married in 1862, but less than three years later his wife Emma filed for divorce. In her petition she claimed that he had committed adultery with Elizabeth Coward, one of the servants, at their residence during the late summer of 1865, on 7th October at Bridgwater, 8th, 9th and 10th at the Saracen's Head, Taunton, on 11th at the Clifton Down Hotel and on the 12th and 13th at Chard's Railway Hotel, Bath. The divorce does not appear to have gone through, but in the 1871 census

Francis Acraman is boarding in East Knoyle, while Emma is at South Cottage, Christchurch Street, with their daughter and son. By 1881 they are back together in Christchurch Street; Francis Acraman was buried at Holy Trinity in 1892, as was Emma in 1917.

The Ilminster connection

In 1827 Lucretia Folkes Bush, daughter of Francis and Lucretia Bush, married Samuel Bush, an attorney. Samuel hailed from Ilminster; for many generations his forefathers worshipped at the Independent Chapel in South Petherton, where Samuel was baptised in 1802. He died scarcely a year after the marriage, and his son Samuel Francis Edgell Bush was born posthumously. He too died young, of consumption, and is remembered in a tablet at St John's. Also baptised at the chapel in South Petherton was Samuel's brother Edwin Bush, the surgeon and apothecary who was featured in FSLS Yearbook 20. In 1829 he was married in Cricklade, to Theodosia White. In 1841 Samuel and Theodosia are in Bruton, together with two 15-year old apprentice surgeons. Also, in the household are Theodosia's widowed mother Elizabeth, Theodosia's brother John White and the latter's wife Amelia, a sister of the Laura Matilda Acraman who had married Francis John Bush. By 1851 Edwin and Theodosia Bush are in Francis Bush's former house in Gentle Street, Frome, together with two daughters, Anne and Lucretia, and Theodosia's mother Elizabeth White. Theodosia's brother John, now a General Practitioner MLCS and Licentiate of Apothecary's Hall, is Behind Town (Christchurch Street) with his wife Amelia, Amelia's sister Emma and the latter's husband and son. The Ilminster Bushes from whom Samuel and Edwin were descended have no clear connection with Francis and Elijah Bush's Kilmersdon/Farmborough branch. There is at least a relationship by marriage, however: Edwin was the brother-in-law of Francis's daughter, and his brother-in-law and colleague, John White, was the brother-in-law of Francis's daughter-in-law!

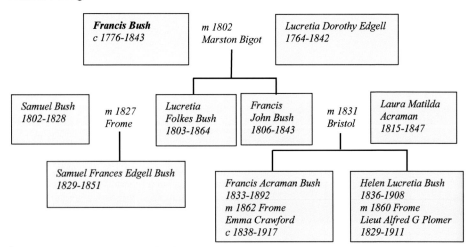

[1] *Frome Portrait, FSLS Yearbook 20, 2017*
[2] *David Smart, FSLS Yearbook 20, 2017*

An Egg that travelled to France and Back

Vida Olive Sheppard was born in August 1902 in Frome and lived all her life in the town. She attended Christ Church School as a child where, in 1915, she and other children in her class were encouraged to help soldiers fighting in the trenches by collecting and sending them gifts, such as small items of food or warm clothing.

Vida Olive Sheppard 1902 - 1977

At the time there was little understanding in Britain of the real nature of trench life on the front line, as information mostly came from letters home and were usually censored before being sent, or from newspaper reports, which never highlighted either heavy losses or the actualities of day-to-day life on the front line. By 1915 the government propaganda machine was getting into its stride and working hard at maintaining public support for the war in all sorts of ways. Posters encouraged recruitment, crucial in the years before the introduction of conscription in 1916, and articles in magazines promoted ways in which families at home could improve the life of the soldier at the front. The postal service was well organised and efficient so parcels containing food and other gifts sent to soldiers were generally quickly delivered and genuinely appreciated by the recipients. This kind of propaganda, which with hindsight can seem simplistic and patronising, was actually quite effective. It was also directed at schools, where many children had fathers, uncles or brothers away on active service.

In this case, the pupils in Vida's class were encouraged to bring to school something that could be sent to the soldiers in France, packed together as a class gift. Vida took an egg as her gift, and the parcel was duly sent off, via one of the well-publicised distribution depots. Vida wrote a message on her egg: 'Vida Olive Sheppard Christ Church School Frome—Health and Luck to dear Tommy Atkins God Bless Him.' Normally, that would have been the end of the matter, however, in this case, the egg was returned, stuffed with cotton wool and carefully packed in a cigarette tin, with a new message: 'Returned with thanks, Pt E Devall, 23.5.15' in blue ink. The sender Private E Devall from the Royal Army Medical Corps No. 12 General Depot, also wrote Vida a letter, explaining that he had received the egg, extracted and enjoyed the contents while carefully preserving the shell and returned it to her as 'a souvenir of this terrible war.' He ended by saying: 'I must conclude thanking you for your kind wishes and please accept the same from me in return.' It has not been possible to identify Private Devall with certainty or establish what happened to him.

The egg after being returned by Private Devall

Vida clearly treasured the egg and all it represented, particularly as her father did serve in France, as a Private in the Army Service Corps. She married Samuel Frederick French at Christ Church in December 1928 and they had one son, Brian who is the proud owner of the egg, a remarkable survivor of the war which gives an unusual insight into life on the Home Front. Brian's mother never told him the story about the egg, and he only heard about it from his father after she died in 1977.

I am grateful to Mary Lynch-Staunton for drawing my attention to this story from 'Antiques Road Show World War One in 100 Family Treasures' by Paul Atterbury. Ed

The Nunney Hoard
by Adrie van der Luijt

The Nunney Hoard of ancient coins was discovered in 1860 and hailed as 'one of the most interesting discoveries of ancient British coins that ever has been placed upon record'[1]. Although mostly forgotten, the Nunney Hoard is an important part of our local heritage. Coins from Nunney are displayed in leading museums across Europe.

The area around Frome has long been of interest to archaeologists. The Frome Hoard was discovered in April 2010 at Witham Friary; it consisted of a ceramic pot 18 inches in diameter filled with 52,503 Roman coins. The hoard is one of the largest ever found in Britain and was acquired by the Museum of Somerset in Taunton, but the Nunney Hoard was certainly no less interesting, albeit less valuable.

On 15 October 1860 two men were ploughing in a field known as the Eleven Acres, part of West Down Farm, (now within the boundaries of a stone quarry) at the far western end of Horn Street in Nunney, when they broke open a small urn filled with coins. The Eleven Acres field is rather higher than the surrounding countryside. The urn was buried in the highest part of the field, at the summit where the depth of soil above the solid rock is six inches to a foot. It is therefore even more remarkable that an urn should have lain undiscovered for so long. It was found less than five yards from where an ancient yew-tree had recently been cut down. The tree may well have been responsible for preserving the hoard. It is also quite possible that the ancient yew-tree, or its predecessor on the spot, may have been the landmark by which whoever buried the treasure, intended to recognise the site later to recover the urn.

The urn seems to have revealed its contents only gradually. The first finders discovered only one or two gold coins; the next man who searched the site found many silver coins, all lying close together but no gold coins at all. A later treasure hunter decided to dig deeper and found several more gold coins together with five or six silver and copper Roman coins.

The men offered some of the coins for sale to three potential buyers:
- Mr Ballard, a silversmith, clock and instrument maker at 21 Bath Street, Frome
- Mr John Webb Singer of Messrs JW Singer & Sons foundry in Frome
- Mr Walker, who had a shop in Harley Street in Bath

An article in the Devizes and Wiltshire Gazette of Thursday 8 November 1860 gives the following information:

'A few days ago, a person offered at the shop of Mr R Walker in Bath two small silver coins, requesting to know their value, mentioning at the same time that he had a considerable quantity at Frome, where he resided. Mr Walker at once pronounced them to be ancient British coins and lost no time in proceeding to Frome to inspect the whole quantity, which he found amounted to 102 silver and two gold pieces, in a fine state of preservation. He made an offer of £16 for the lot, which sum was ultimately accepted.

On making enquiries at the silversmiths in the town, Mr Walker likewise found at Mr Ballard's 70 other silver coins of similar character. It appears that as some labourers were ploughing in a field at Holwell, near Nunney, the ploughshare struck upon an earthen pan and scattered its contents; the men, not knowing the value of such curious articles, sold them again in the village, for a trifle.

On questioning them Mr Ballard and Mr Walker arrived at a correct knowledge of the number of coins found: 10 gold and 202 silver; of these, eight gold and 30 silver are missing, and are now being traced. The rest of the find Mr Walker has secured.

The owner of the farm not only allowed the coins he had kept for himself to be examined but gave permission for a detailed search on the site. Six more silver coins were subsequently found.

The silver coins are chiefly alike, each having a horse impressed on the reverse, and a rude head on the obverse. There are, however, names on some of these new to numismatics, and Mr Walker has very properly placed the whole in the hands of the authorities at the British Museum.'

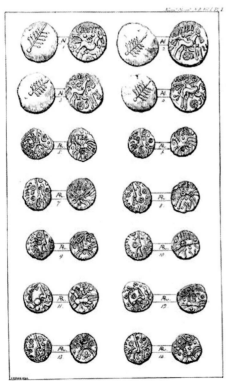

BRITISH COINS FOUND AT NUNNEY NEAR FROME. 1860.

Mr Walker may well have handed the coins over to the British Museum, but they did not end up there, at least not until much later. In 1860 the British Museum trustees decided to divide up the Department of Antiquities and create a new Department of Coins and Medals. In fact, most of the coins were sold, to Captain (later Sir) Roderick Murchison and Sir John Evans, both members of the Royal Numismatic Society and passionate collectors of ancient British coins. As collectors, they had relatively few serious competitors during the 1850s and early 1860s. Although there were other members of the Numismatic Society, most of them did not have the same obsessive drive to collect.

Evans often mentioned Murchison in his correspondence, for example in the letters of JW Singer, who was trying to secure coins from the Nunney Hoard for Evans: 'Captain Murchison asks a pretty good price for his; I will only say that

Capt M lately charged 10/- for two of them to a dealer.'

Sir John Evans (1823-1908) was for many years, manager of the large paper mill of his uncle, and later father-in-law, John Dickinson at Nash Mills, Hemel Hempstead, but he was particularly distinguished as an antiquary, archaeologist and numismatist, indeed he was the first person to devise a systematic classification of British Iron Age coinage and served as President of the Royal Numismatic Society for over 25 years.

Evans kept no catalogue of his collection, so it is uncertain whether he bought Murchison's coins from the Nunney Hoard. In 1864 he published 'Coins of the Ancient Britons'; it frequently mentions the Nunney coins referring to 'the hoard found at Nunney'. The book was the first standard work on ancient British coins, illustrated with engravings of 355 coins. The book became the reference for the classification of British Iron Age coins, although it was subsequently found to be wrong on minor points, mainly caused by later finds; most of his material is still valid today after over 150 years.

Although Sir John Evans was a passionate collector of ancient British coins, he was clearly excited to have obtained coins from the Nunney Hoard. On 13 December 1860, he addressed a meeting of the Numismatic Society in London: 'By the kind co-operation of Captain Murchison, I am enabled to communicate to the Numismatic Society an account of one of the most interesting discoveries of ancient British coins that ever has been placed upon record. Although not in intrinsic value coming near some of the various hoards which have formerly been discovered yet, so far as concerns the information to be derived from the coins themselves, and those of Roman mintage, with which they were found associated, the present find is entitled to take at least equal rank with the celebrated finds of High Wycombe, Farley Heath, Almondsbury, Whaddon Chase, or Weston, if it is not even of more importance.'

A detailed analysis of what is known of the find in 1860 is given as follows: 'The plough had shattered the urn in which the Nunney Hoard coins were found so badly that only a few small pieces of it could be recovered. Little is known about its form except that it was round with sides that sloped outwards. It had an exterior diameter of about 4.5 inches at its base and was made of very imperfectly burnt clay. One clue that it was made locally was a fossil shell, *Rhynconella concinna,* commonly found in local limestone that was embedded at the bottom of the urn. A small bow-shaped brooch, a fibula, was also found on the site, but it is not certain whether this was linked to the urn. A total 249 coins from the Nunney Hoard were recovered: 10 British gold coins, 232 British silver coins, 3 silver and 4 brass Roman coins. About 23 were minted by Antedrigus, 27 by a chief whose name probably begins with Eisu, two bear the name or part of a name Catti, the remainder are without inscription, which is typical of British coins before the Roman invasion. The Roman coins are from the reign of the Emperor Claudius (41-54 AD).

Roman Republican coins circulated for a long period in Britain due to their high silver content. It is quite common for them to occur in a hoard with Iron Age or Roman silver coins. It is difficult to establish exactly when the Nunney Hoard was put in the ground based on dating the coins alone. Although the Roman coins can be dated to Claudius and other emperors, they had clearly been in circulation for some time after they were struck.'

Sir John Evans described the Roman coins of Claudius as exhibiting wear consistent with eight to ten years of constant circulation. Among the Nunney coins was a silver denarius, thought to have been minted under Julius Caesar around 48BC, showing an elephant trampling a serpent.

According to Mr Singer a coin of Caligula was also discovered: a *denarius* in reasonable state from around 37 AD showing the head of Caligula on one side and that of Augustus on the other.

The Nunney Hoard also included what were possibly the earliest coins minted in Somerset, those bearing the name Antedragus which were made from very poor metal. He was most likely a chief of the *Dubonni* tribes, as the inhabitants of Somerset were called. He was probably succeeded by Eisu, while Catti was another *Dubonni* leader mentioned on coins found in Nunney. The owner may have buried his coins when the Romans came to conquer Somerset between 50-55 AD, left to fight them and never returned. Over 1,800 years elapsed before his money was recovered.

After Sir John's death, his very large personal archaeological collection passed to his son Sir Arthur John Evans (1851-1941), archaeologist and keeper of the Ashmolean Museum at Oxford from 1884-1908 who gave most of the collection to the Ashmolean Museum, however, in 1919 Sir Arthur donated his father's collection of ancient coins to the British Museum.

As a result, much of the Nunney Hoard is now in the archives of the British Museum. Some coins are in the University Museum in Leeds, one silver coin of Antedragus is in the Museum of Somerset in Taunton together with a coin of Catti (according to Evans), but this has been called into question.

About half a dozen coins from the Nunney Hoard have been reported in the Holburne Museum in Bath. Others belonged to collector and Liverpudlian shipowner Richard Cyril Lockett; they were auctioned in April 1960, when the British Museum bought 51 Anglo-Saxon and Norman coins, however, the 34 coins from the Nunney Hoard in the British Museum's online catalogue came from the collection of Sir John Evans.

That number is only a fraction of the 249 coins in the Nunney hoard, and, despite extensive research, it remains unclear what happened with the rest. Dr Eleanor Ghey from the Department of Portable Antiquities and Treasure at the British Museum reported: 'I think the short answer is that we will never fully know the whereabouts of all the coins, or how many were in the hoard when found. Ones that have passed into museum collections have often lost their provenance by that stage. We also find that not all the coins were reported to the authorities in this period.' Philip de Jersey has researched the hoard and makes the total number of coins he can associate with the hoard to be 254.He used the Evans archive at the Ashmolean to trace correspondence about the hoard and concluded that 'finds evidently continued for some years afterwards, and it is difficult to estimate what the original total might have been'. He does list some coins from the Fitzwilliam, Ashmolean, Leeds University collections and some in Paris at the Bibliotheque Nationale but was unable to trace the coins in Bath. Catrin Jones, Curator of Decorative Arts at the Holburne Museum in Bath, stated: 'I can confirm that, what I think are 6 coins from the Nunney Hoard, are still part of the Holburne Museum's collection. They were part of Sir William Holburne's bequest to the museum. They are described as 'one of six Romano British Coins (found at Frome 1860) Tribe *Dubonnni*, Obverse Crude head with ornaments right. Reverse: Triple tailed horse (modelled on Belgic coinage). Unfortunately we don't have any further information about the coins.'

A MOST interesting discovery of ancient British coins has just been made in a field at Hollwell, the property of Mr. Glencross. The coins were in a small vase, or urn, of very coarse material, which was broken entirely to pieces in ploughing the land, and the contents were thus brought to light. There were about 200 silver coins and 10 gold ones, and although their intrinsic value is only about £3, yet from their great rarity they are of much interest. We believe there never was such a find of coins of this kind before, for with rare exceptions they are only met with in the neighbourhood of Frome, and their importance may be judged of when we state that one was picked up in this town and once sold as a button, realized a high price at a sale in London, and was taken to France to enrich the collection of the government. But of the number now found none will reach so high a figure again. We trust no unwise interference of the police, nor of any other party, will prevent the recovery of every one of these coins, as they are of great interest in throwing light upon obscure parts of archaeology. The greater number of the coins have been sold to a dealer in Bath for £10, but a few may be seen at Mr. Singer's, Market Place.

Frome Times report October 1860

On Friday 2 December 1955 a coin was found in Westbury-on-Trym, Bristol and now in the Bristol Museum, that experts believe was created using the same dies as some of the coins found in the Nunney Hoard. A copper alloy *nummus* of the House of Constantine, CONSTANTINOPOLIS, Victory on prow reverse, mint unclear, AD 330-40, was found in Nunney on 26 August 2010 with a metal detector, while the coin found at Westbury-on-Trym had the same disjointed horse and wheel on one side, with the letter ANTEDRIG, and the usual piece of bracken (or pine-tree, fish bone or ear of corn) on the back.

The increased use of metal detectors in recent decades has greatly expanded the number of coin hoard finds – there are around 340 Iron Age coin hoards and some 2700 Roman coin hoards currently recorded across Britain, increasing at around 80 a year. Over 600 coin hoards are known from the second half of the 3rd century, the largest number from any period of British history, and also more hoards from the period than from anywhere else in the Roman Empire. Ancient coins are also still being found by local enthusiasts with metal detectors around Nunney and Holwell. Every find is carefully reported and catalogued by the Portal Antiquities Scheme, whose online database finds.org.uk included Roman and Byzantine coins discovered in Nunney.

[1] *Sir John Evans, Address to the Royal Numismatic Society, London, 13 December 1860*

This is an abridged version of a longer article by Adrie van der Luijt on the Visit Nunney website. Ed

My thanks to Mick Davis for this delightful membership card of the Frome Baths Committee & Swimming Club of 1913. Ed

Rough Music - somewhere near Frome in 1766

To the PRINTER of the Bath Chronicle

Sir

Last Easter Monday a numerous and extraordinary Mob assembled in a little Parish about three Miles West of Frome, composed entirely of Rogues, Whores, and Bastards to execute in Effigy their late Overseer. The Crime laid to his Charge was, that he had made it a standing Rule, during the Time of being in his Office, for the Father of every Bastard Child to do something, if able, towards Maintenance. Those of the Mob of most Note, were the Hangman, the Postillion (as they call'd him) to the Hangman, the Devil and the Parson. The Hangman had been lately taken up for a Bastard; the Postillion a nog-headed Boy about Ten Years of Age, is the fourth Child of a virtuous single woman. This chaste Mother is the Bastard of a Gipsy, and dropt about thirty Years ago in the Porch of a poor Woman, as a present to the Parish, and now lives with a young Fellow, as a necessary Piece of Furniture, in a little paultry Ale House. The Devil has been a dev'lish Whore-Master, and the Parson's Morals stand pretty near on the same Footing. These four, I am told, were the principal Actors; the Procession began about Four o'Clock, (whilst the Vestry were choosing new Officers) and those that were not furnis'd with Cow-Horns, Sheep-Bells, Brass Pans, Frying-Pans and the like agreeable Music assisted with Hooting, Screaming and Yelling, all the Way to the Gallows, where being arrived, and Silence demanded, the mock Parson began to exhort the Criminal, and the Audience, in a Manner suitable to the Occasion. This being finished, the Hangman proceeded to Execution: the Effigy, after hanging a proper Time, was cut down, and carefully laid in a Coffin, and, then delivered to the Undertaker. The Undertaker, when going off, was met by the Devil, and after a terrible Conflict, was robbed of his Charge.

Thus ended this very ridiculous Affair. It is surprising no Mischief was done, as the Mob in general were very drunk; but I don't hear of any, except the burning of a very good Greatcoat of the honest drunken Farmer's that lent them his Cart, and the singeing of a small Matter of the Gown and Cassock of the mock Parson.

I am, Sir, Yours, etc BW

My thanks to Clive Wilkins for this letter to Pope's Bath Chronicle, 17 April 1766. Ed

Riot in Beckington, 1766

Early Thursday Morning a large Mob of poor People, consisting of nearly two Thousand, went to North Bradley Mill and pulled down part of it; broke all the Windows of the house and Mill, and shared what Corn they found there amongst themselves. From whence they proceeded to Beckington Mill, near Frome. The Owner of the Mill, having been inform'd of their coming a few Hours before applied to Thomas Prowse Esq, one of the Representatives of this County, and several other Gentlemen, who gave the Mob a Meeting at Beckington Turnpike. Mr Prowse made a very pathetic Speech on the Occasion, he laid before them the dangerous Consequences of such rash Proceedings, desiring them to disperse, and he would do what lay in his Power for their immediate Relief. They replied, they might as well be hang'd as starv'd to Death; many of them declar'd they had not eat a Morsel of Bread for three Days, but had subsisted on Grains &c, others appeared so very feeble thro' Want of Food, that they could scarce crawl, and told the Gentlemen that their *leoffer'd* them Money to purchase Provisions, and told them the Parish should take Care of their Families, but all had no Effect on the Mob, they were determin'd to proceed and accordingly march'd up to the Mill.

The Miller having provided himself with Fire-Arms and proper Assistance, kept continually firing at the Mob, and slightly wounding some, it so exasperated them, that having procured some Fire-Arms, a terrible Battle ensued, which lasted a considerable Time, and a great Number of the Rioters were wounded, many of them dangerously; one is since dead, and 'tis said some others cannot recover. Their Ammunition being expended, the Mob made a large Fire in the Field, then flung the lighted Firebrands all about, which set Fire to a Faggot-Pile, a Rick of Hay about twelve Ton, the Stable, the Dwelling House and Mill; the People in the Mill narrowly escaped being kill'd, some of them jump'd into the River and swam across; others mix'd with the Rioters, and so escap'd in the Confusion.

The Mob took all the Wheat and Flour they could see, and divided it amongst themselves, then wheeling the Miller's Waggon into the Fire, and burning all the sacks they cou'd find, they went off. As soon as they were gone, the People in the Neighbourhood exerted themselves in extinguishing the Flames and saved the Stable, Mill and Waggon, but all the rest were entirely destroy'd.

My thanks to Clive Wilkins for this article from Pope's Bath Chronicle, 25 September, 1766. Ed

John Wesley's Journal: Frome

March 1753
Wed 14 I preached at Frome, a dry, barren, uncomfortable place. The congregation at Shaftesbury in the evening were of a more excellent spirit.

John Wesley portrait
Allan R Bevere

September 1753
Mon 10 I preached to the condemned malefactors in Newgate; but I could make little impression upon them. I then took horse for Paulton, where I called on Stephen Plummer, once of our society, but now a zealous Quaker. He was much pleased with my calling, and came to hear me preach. Being straitened for time, I concluded sooner than usual; but as soon as I had done, Stephen began. After I had listened half an hour, finding he was no nearer the end, I rose up to go away. His sister then begged him to leave off; on which he flew into a violent rage, and roared louder and louder, till an honest man took him in his arms, and gently carried him away. What a wise providence was it, that this poor young man turned Quaker, some years before he ran mad! So the honor of turning his brain now rests upon them, which otherwise must have fallen upon the Methodists. I preached at six in the evening at Buckland, about two miles from Frome, in a meadow of Mr Emblen's, a wonderful monument of the grace of God; who, from the day he received peace, being then acquainted with no Methodist, has continually walked in the light of God's countenance. The Curate had provided a mob, with horns, and other things convenient, to prevent the congregation's hearing me. But the better half of the mob soon left their fellows, and listened with great attention. The rest did no harm: So that we had a comfortable opportunity; and another at five in the morning.

November 1759
Mon 22 I left Bristol, and having preached at Shepton, Coleford, Frome, and Salisbury in my way.

September 1763

Thur 8 At nine I preached in the same place, to a far more serious audience. Between eleven and twelve I preached at Westcomb, and in the evening at Frome. How zealous to hear are these people; and yet how little do they profit by hearing! I think this will not always be the case. By and by we shall rejoice over them.

October 1766

Sun 28 I preached in Princes Street at eight, in Kingswood at two, and at five near the new Square. The last especially was an acceptable time; particularly while I was explaining, "Neither can they die any more; but are the children of God, being children of the resurrection." In the following days I preached at Pensford, Paulton, Coleford, Buckland, Frome, Beckington, Freshford, and Bradford.

September 1767

Wed 23 About noon I preached at Buckland, and in the evening at Frome: But the House was too small, so that many were constrained to go away. So the next evening I preached in a meadow, where a multitude, of all denominations, attended. It seems that God is at length giving a more general call to this town also; the people whereof seemed before, in every sense, to be "rich and increased in goods, and having need of nothing."

September 1768

Thur 29 I rode to Frome. The people here seem more alive than most I have seen in the circuit; and this is the more strange, because in this town only there is such a mixture of men of all opinions: Anabaptists, Quakers, Presbyterians, Arians, Antinomians, Moravians, and what not. If any hold to the truth, in the midst of all these, surely the power must be of God.

Friday 30 we observed as a day of fasting and prayer; and it was a good day for many, who no sooner called, than God answered them in the joy of their heart.

September 1770

Tues 11 In the evening I preached at Frome; but not abroad, as I designed, because of the rain. The next evening I preached in the adjoining meadow, to as quiet a congregation as that in the House.

October 1775

On Tuesday I went on to Bristol. On Thursday and Friday, I preached at Keynsham, Bradford, and Bath; on Tuesday, 19, at Frome; and on Wednesday, at Pensford.

September 1776

Wed 11 I preached about one at Bath; and about six, in a meadow, near the preaching-house, in Frome, besought a listening multitude "not to receive the grace of God in vain."

September 1778
Tues 8 In the evening I stood on one side of the market-place at Frome, and declared to a very numerous congregation, "His commandments are not grievous." They stood as quiet as those at Bristol, a very few excepted; most of whom were, by the courtesy of England, called Gentlemen. How much inferior to the keelmen and colliers!

September 1779
Mon 13 I preached at Bath and Bradford; on Tuesday, at the end of the new House, in Frome.

John Wesley preaching   *Methodist Church Archives*

October 1779
Fri 24 James Gerrish, jun, of Roade, near Frome, was for several years zealous for God: But he too grew rich, and grew lukewarm, till he was seized with a consumption. At the approach of death he was "horribly afraid;" he was "in the lowest darkness, and in the deep." But "he cried unto God in his trouble," and was "delivered out of his distress." He was filled with peace and joy unspeakable and so continued till he went to God. His father desired I would preach his funeral sermon; which I accordingly did this day, at Roade. I concluded the busy day with a comfortable watch-night at Kingswood.

September 1781

Mon 10 I preached at Paulton and Shepton-Mallet to a lively, increasing people in each place.

Tuesday, 11 I found the same cause of rejoicing at Coleford; and the next evening at Frome.

September 1782

Mon 9 About nine I preached at Paulton, where the flame is abated, but not quenched. The same is the case at Shepton-Mallet, where I preached in the evening.

Tuesday 10 I went on to the simple-hearted colliers, at Coleford, abundance of whom met at six in the evening, in a green meadow, which was delightfully gilded by the rays of the setting sun.

Wednesday 11 I preached to a large and serious congregation at the end of the preaching-house at Frome.

September 1784

Tues 14 I preached at Bath and Bradford;
Wednesday 15 at Trowbridge and Frome.

September 1785

Tues 6 I preached at Paulton and Coleford;

Wednesday 7 in an open place near the road, at Mells. Just as I began, a wasp, though unprovoked, stung me upon the lip. I was afraid it would swell, so as to hinder my speaking; but it did not. I spoke distinctly, near two hours in all; and was no worse for it. In the evening I preached with much satisfaction at Frome, to a mixed multitude of rich and poor; and afterwards strongly exhorted them that had believed to walk in love, after the example of our Great Master.

September 1788

Thursday 11 We had a lovely congregation at Frome, both in the evening and at five in the morning. At length this wilderness, too, as it has long appeared to be, begins to blossom and bud as the rose.

September 1789

Thursday 17 I preached at Frome, to a much larger audience, and with much of the presence of God.

I am grateful to Peter Clark for these extracts from John Wesley's Journal. Ed

Oxley's Colliery, Buckland Dinham

The *Frome Times* of 11 March 1874 reported that preliminary borings for coal were carried out at Buckland Dinham by the Diamond Boring Company for Mr J Oxley of Frome which were sufficiently successful to justify the sinking of a shaft. The site is about half a mile south of the village in the valley between Barrow Hill and a track leading to Mells, hence in an advantageous position to the Radstock Railway.

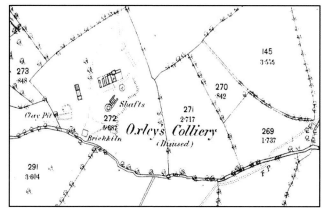

Extract from 1885 Edition 1 : 25000 Map   *Oxley's Colliery Chimney*

Although no coal was extracted owing to flooding of the shaft, the *Somerset Guardian* of 14 October 1910 reported that borings were being carried out on a disused shaft at Buckland Dinham in the hope of finding coal there. In November 1924, the *Somerset Standard* stated that several cottages had been bought and pulled down in about 1880 to prevent the village from becoming a 'mining village', however, the work at the pit proved unsuccessful, the means for pumping out the water being inadequate.

In 1956 the National Coal Board stated that the two shafts were probably sunk about 1880 to work the coal seams of the Lower Coal Series. The shafts were 12 feet in diameter and were abandoned in very highly inclined formations at a depth of 140 yards. The shafts have been sealed with reinforced concrete covers.

After nearly 150 years the chimney built of stone and brick stands on the side of the hill as a striking record of the mine that never was. The bricks for the upper section of the chimney were made on site.

Fred Chant[1] has recorded his childhood memories of the chimney.

[1] *FSLS Yearbook 6, 1995-6*

I am grateful to Gerald Quartley for the information on Oxley's Colliery. Ed

Frome Society Diamond Jubilee, Selwood School, 13 October 2018
by Hilary Daniel

Hilary Daniel

Sixty years is a long, long time, but the first evening of our dear Society is still very clear to my memory. There was a real crowd here in this hall on 9 October 1958, all 'the great and the good' of Frome, as one might say. Sir Leonard Woolley, probably the greatest archaeologist of his day, the man who had excavated the fabulous Ur of the Chaldees in Mesopotamia, was here to give us his blessing, at the invitation of the irrepressible Eunice Overend, who knew everybody! The chairman was the kindly headmaster of the old Frome Grammar School, Gilbert Fairs, and I was beside him in support, with the duty of presenting the proposed rules and constitution and taking notes of the proceedings. Everything went off exactly to plan, to found what was then to be known simply as 'The Frome Society', which was approved with acclamation.

In those days historic houses and ancient town centres were little thought of. Most of the war damage in the cities and urban areas had already been patched up, and there was a countrywide drive to bring in the new: new shopping centres, new housing estates, new roads and new transport systems. Anybody who hankered after old things was derided as out-of-date and hindering Progress. All over the kingdom great country houses were being pulled down by owners who could not afford their upkeep, and town councils were competing with one another as to how many so-called 'housing units' they could put up in a year, in an orgy of what was called 'slum clearance'. The whole character of most of our historic cities and market towns was suddenly in danger, and when it was announced that the Frome Urban District Council, too, was being approached by various developers who had their eyes on the whole charming and ancient Trinity area, some of our townspeople were stirred into action.

In 1956 Peter Belham, a distinguished local historian, and HJ Norville, a photographer, put on an exhibition of items of historic interest in St John's School, which first drew the attention of many of us to some of the treasures that had, unnoticed, surrounded us as we grew up. This began to focus our attention to the threat to the Trinity area, and in July 1958 a handful of us met at my home to discuss what we could do to prevent the tight-knit communities that had grown up in the old clothworkers' cottages from being superseded into stark new estates of faceless flats and our picturesque marketplace and shopping streets from being replaced with the rows of uniform ugly concrete commercial development that had already taken over the centres of so many other small towns.

We went further; noting that the area around Stonebridge was already being developed for new families coming into the town; we had the idea that our new fellow-townspeople might appreciate some means of learning something of the history and amenities of this part of Somerset. We suggested forming a Society that would act as a repository for information, records and education about all aspects of Frome and its surroundings, not only its history, but also its geology, botany, architecture, biology: in fact, anything and everything that made our town what it was and what it is.

This idea seemed to catch on, and everyone we talked to seemed enthusiastic and supportive, but we were not really prepared for the size of the audience that turned up to the initial public meeting in this hall. Still we plunged in, learning as we went, and the town supported us all the way. We originally had three separate sections, for history, geology and natural history, and we did not simply sit down and listen to lectures or go out on carefully organised sightseeing trips: under the enthusiastic leadership of the mercurial Eunice Overend, we did archaeological digs, nature study walks, and restoration projects like the clearance of the brambles and other undergrowth then defacing Vallis Vale. Early AGMs regularly made mention of thirty or more activities in every year. I have been delighted to see that under Julian Watson's chairmanship recently, there has been a movement to restore some of the active aspects of the Society's work.

As the Society grew, it quickly became recognised as embodying both brain and muscle working for the improvement of Frome. We were still quite new when the Frome UDC requested us to set up a museum, first at Church Steps, later in Wine Street and finally in North Parade. Concern about the future of the town as well as about its past led us to sponsor the Civic Society, which now works comfortably alongside us. Concern about the sorry state of some of our ancient buildings gave rise to the founding of the Frome Historic Buildings Trust, which over a number of years, was able to juggle grants and the goodwill of interested parties, to restore a useful number of ancient buildings to habitable condition that would otherwise have crumbled away. With the price of property reaching current insane heights, that pattern of working is sadly no longer practicable, but the Trust's accumulated funds have been distributed among similar worthy projects.

Before ending, I must name a few personalities, and these are mostly people from the past whom many of you will not have known: Eunice Overend, that energetic polymath, has already been mentioned; Hilda Massey was a meticulous collector of records in the early days. Laurie Bowring was the Chairman for over two decades, and he set the pattern of activities that we follow to this day. We owe an enormous dept to our distinguished quartet of historians: Peter Belham, Derek Gill, Rodney Goodall and Michael McGarvie, the first three sadly no longer with us, but Michael very much alive and welcome here today as our President. Finally, I come to Katharine Ashworth, a most remarkable person. She was the daughter of Alice Seeley, Lady Harris, educated in Frome, prominent Congo missionary in whose honour the Society erected a plaque last year. Katharine, to whom I was solicitor, was a generous lady and altogether larger than life. Often flamboyantly dressed, she dominated any company she graced, and she loved the grand gesture. When I told her about the Frome Society, and that the new Museum needed to find larger premises, she immediately showed intense interest, having purchased Wine Street House in a fit of nostalgia, which had been the site of the school she had attended when very

young. Not knowing quite what to do with it, she thereupon offered to lease it to the Frome Society as our headquarters and as a home for the Museum; the rent she required was, typically romantic: a red rose once a year! In her will she left the freehold of Wine Street House to our Society, and that was the source of the funds which now enable us to make grants for new publications and to subsidise some of our members' activities. I trust that we shall always remember to place a red rose on her grave in the Dissenters Cemetery on her birthday. We owe so much to so many worthy members.

Of recent years, you are all aware that this Society has been growing at an amazing rate. With over 450 members, we are quite a social force in the town and seem destined before long to outgrow all available venues for our meetings. We are, I am afraid, a little more passive and sedentary than we were in the early days; it is no

Peter Clark placing the rose on Katharine Ashworth's grave on 21 June 2014

secret that our average age is rather advanced, and that our overall colouring is predominantly grey, but we are indeed fulfilling a very useful, indeed a vital role, and I am extremely proud to have been associated with the Society from its very early days.

Start planning now for our 70th!

Members who are interested in the first 15 years of FSLS can find them in 'The Future of the Past' by Douglas Twelvetrees (FSLS 1974). Ed